UNDER A KANSAS MOON

The Final Chapter

TOMMY & HILDE WILKENS

TOMMY & HILDE WILKENS

Printed in the United States of America
First Printing 2021
First Edition 2021

10 9 8 7 6 5 4 3 2 1

Dedication

We would like to dedicate this book to the late author/poet Paul Foreman of Austin, Texas. Without Paul's years of friendship and encouragement and guidance and his ever-dedicated support to our writing, this work would never have been possible. We would also like to thank Ken Dixon of Deltona, Florida for his professional editing skills and his friendship. And we offer this book in loving memory of Frans Vanrenterghem and Huguette Snoeck of Avelgem, Belgium.

TABLE OF CONTENTS

INTRODUCTION

In this book, we detail the true story of how convicted murderers Richard Hickock and Perry Smith spent their last years on death row trying to avoid their execution at the Kansas State Penitentiary (now the Lansing Correctional Facility) – often referred to as the Kansas death house. Our extensive research has revealed many new and intriguing facts regarding the killers' capture, the highly-publicized murder trial, the many desperate attempts to have their convictions overturned, and – finally – the day they paid the ultimate price.

Much of this information has never before been compiled and published. It's a fascinating tale – one that explores in great detail both the workings of the criminal mind and the many ways in which our legal system can be used to delay and deflect the best efforts of society to exact rightful punishment for even the most heinous of crimes.

Tommy and Hilde Wilkens

CHAPTER 1

Holcomb, Kansas, a mere 70 miles from the Colorado border, was a small town born near railroad tracks that ran through the western wheat plains. Incorporated in 1909, it was named for a local rancher, D. C. Holcomb. A sugar beet processing plant provided much of the local employment. Further growth soon brought a new U. S. Post Office to town, followed in 1912 by the establishment of the Holcomb State Bank at the corner of Main Street and Douglas Avenue.

Like residents of so many other small farm communities that dotted the Midwestern states, Holcomb's citizens took great pride in their heritage. Most lived according the Christian faith, building a strong tradition of deep family ties and good, hard, honest work. The town was thriving by 1949 - but with just 270 residents, it was still barely on the map.

Soon, wheat farming and cattle ranching were playing a major role in keeping Holcomb afloat. With new prosperity came several churches, a hardware store, a market, and Bess Hartman's cafe. The Hartman Cafe quickly became a meeting place for locals. It wasn't much – just four small tables and a counter that developed worn and rounded edges over the years from the regulars pushing up against it.

Hartman Cafe

You could smell the freshly brewed coffee as soon as you walked in. That, plus soft drinks, sandwiches, and 3.2 beer were pretty much the whole menu, and it never changed. At the Hartman Cafe, you'd sit and sip and hear the local gossip. It was simple, innocent, small-town America. Crime was almost nonexistent.

The bank had been robbed, of course. In fact, it happened twice – in 1917 and again in 1930. Both times, the notorious Fleagle gang was responsible. Brothers Ralph, Fred, Little Jake and Walter got $1500 the first time, but the amount of their second take has been lost to antiquity. They were outsiders, and most people who resided in Holcomb knew and trusted one another. During their evening walks, windows were left open and doors remained unlocked. Life in Holcomb was good.

On a cold November night in 1959, everything changed. Like a biting winter wind sweeping across the prairie, evil in its very darkest form invaded the peaceful little town under a Kansas moon, spreading horror and terror the likes of which could not have been imagined even one day before.

That fateful night, four members of Holcomb's most beloved family – the Clutters - were brutally murdered.

The Clutter Family

Herbert Clutter was a highly-respected community leader. In 1954, he'd been appointed by President Dwight D. Eisenhower to serve on the Federal Farm Credit Board, and he was the founder of the Kansas Association of Wheat Growers. He'd been the President of the National Wheat Growers Association, a Sunday school teacher, and the successful owner and operator of River Valley Farms.

"Herb" Clutter, his wife Bonnie Mae, daughter Nancy Mae, and young Kenyon Neal Clutter were known to be kind and gentle folk, loved and respected by their neighbors. Within hours, the horrible news had spread like a flood and genuine fear gripped the people. Doors that normally stood open were now shut and windows were latched tight. Suspicion ran wild. Local and national media were converging on the town, hungry for information. Life as residents had known it was suddenly lost forever.

The cold-blooded killings were a shock to America's national innocence regarding such matters. Until then, it had been accepted as gospel that such things happened in large cities and densely populated areas. Now, the worst of the worst had come to little Holcomb, Kansas. There was no way to process an event of that magnitude without having a basis for comparison, and none existed. The country now had to accept a new reality – that unspeakable evil could strike anywhere at any time, targeting even the innocent. The murders changed everything, and they would have a long-lasting impact.

The effect on Holcomb was profound. Those who viewed the aftermath of the slaughter found that details replayed in their minds like a film they couldn't stop watching. Because of the sheer violence and brutality of the killings, the Clutter murder scene would go down in history as one of the worst in the history of both Kansas and the United States. Now, decades later, people all over the world can view for themselves what the cameras' lenses captured and form their own thoughts. The macabre images, preserved for all time, leave an inescapable message for all who choose to look: It could happen to you.

After a two-month-long nationwide manhunt by agents of the Kansas Bureau of Investigation and the FBI, the suspected killers of the four Clutter family members were finally apprehended. They had fled across the country and slipped into Mexico, only to return to Las Vegas and be captured there. Now the state of Kansas was prepared to see that justice was done. And in the minds of most that meant - after a trial - death by hanging.

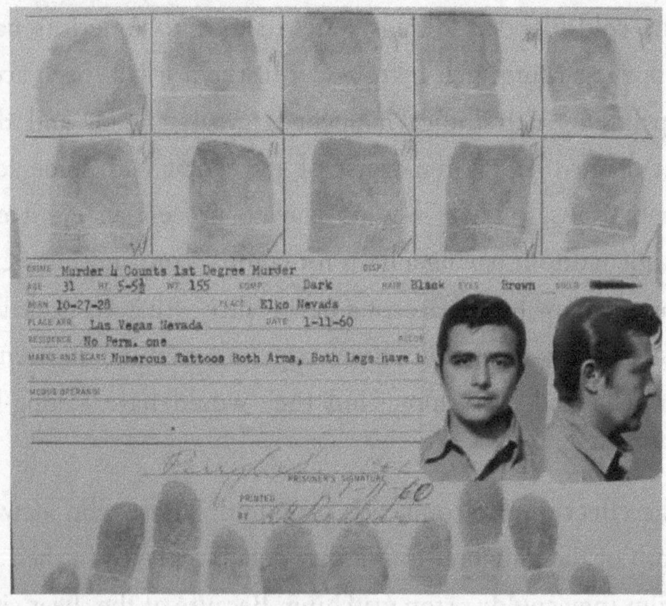
CRIME Murder 4 Counts 1st Degree Murder
AGE 31 HT 5-5½ WT 155 COMP Dark HAIR Black EYES Brown
BORN 10-27-28 PLACE Elko Nevada
PLACE ARR Las Vegas Nevada DATE 1-11-60
RESIDENCE No Perm. one
MARKS AND SCARS Numerous Tattoos Both Arms, Both Legs have b
MODUS OPERANDI
PRISONER'S SIGNATURE
PRINTED BY

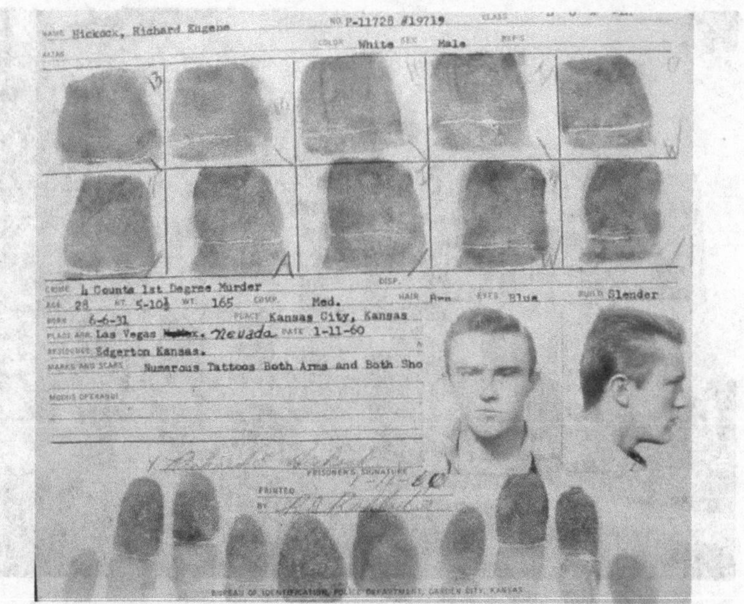

Name: Hickock, Richard Eugene
No. P-11728 #19719
Color: White Sex: Male

Crime: 4 Counts 1st Degree Murder
Age: 28 Ht. 5-10½ Wt. 165 Comp. Med. Eyes: Blue Build: Slender
Born: 6-6-31 Place: Kansas City, Kansas
Place Arr.: Las Vegas, Nevada Date: 1-11-60
Residence: Edgerton Kansas.
Marks and Scars: Numerous Tattoos Both Arms and Both Sho
Modus Operandi:
Prisoner's Signature
Printed By
Bureau of Identification, Police Department, Garden City, Kansas

The crime and the subsequent trial would be described in great detail by author Truman Capote in his non-fiction novel <u>In Cold Blood</u>. It covered the quadruple murders and the capture and trials of the accused and went on to become one of the greatest non-fiction books of modern times, selling more than a million hard copies and over 11 million more copies in paperback. <u>In Cold Blood</u> was published in 32 languages and sold well around the world, with over 700,000 copies purchased in Germany alone.

We'll dig deeper here, unearthing new information about the five years convicted killers Richard "Dick" Hickock and Perry Edward Smith spent on death row trying to appeal their convictions. The book is based on our research at the Kansas Historical Society's state archives, Kansas State Penitentiary official records, and other related historical documentation preserved for review.

Our story begins the morning of March 22, 1960, at the Finney County Courthouse in Garden City, Kansas. The trial of Richard Hickock and Perry Smith would be like none other held there since it was built in 1928. It was the case that would put the town and the state on the front pages of newspapers throughout the United States. Garden City was the center of the action.

Barber shops, little cafes, hotels and other local businesses accustomed to serving only locals were now overflowing with people from all over Kansas and around the country. On the first morning of the trial, the crowd in the courtroom included 150 potential jurors and representatives of both regional and national news media. The trial would be presided over by the honorary Judge Roland H. Tate. There were only four women in the large jury pool: Mrs. Kathleen Bruchy, Miss Amy Gillespie, Mrs. E. Mearl Hutton, and Violet McElroy. None of them was chosen to serve.

Judge Roland H. Tate

Everyone who entered was checked by the Kansas State Police, and once the space was filled to capacity the doors were closed and then guarded. Inside, District Court Clerk Mae Purdy, in a loud, commanding voice, called out the names of the twelve jurors and two alternates. Each of them stood to be recognized and stepped forward. Judge Tate laid out his rules: No smoking or standing in the aisles. Seats designated for the press were to be used only by the press. No cameras or recordings of any kind would be permitted. There would be no interviews within the courtroom. And the proceedings would be conducted in an orderly fashion.

At 10:04 AM, Richard Hickock was brought in, handcuffed to Sheriff Wendle Meier. The defendant was dressed in brown trousers, a white shirt with a brown tie and highly polished brown shoes, and white socks. Moments later, Perry Smith arrived, similarly handcuffed to Deputy Sheriff Micky Hawkins. With his coal black hair neatly combed, the five-foot, three-inch Smith was dressed in blue dungarees with the pants cuffs rolled up, a white shirt open at the neck, and white socks and spit-shined black shoes.

Perry Smith

Seated at the prosecution's table was County Attorney Duane West. A lifelong resident of Garden City, West had graduated from Garden City High School and Washburn College. Assisting in the prosecution would be Logan Green. Originally from Kentucky, he had served as Finney County Attorney from 1935 to 1943.

At the defense table was Hickock's representative, Harrison Smith. A local attorney, Smith had worked in the Finney County court system for over ten years and was a graduate of the University of Kansas Law School. He had served in the United States Navy and was originally from Racine, Wisconsin. Perry Smith would be represented by Arthur Fleming, a local Garden City resident and the town's former Mayor. He had also been President of the local school board. Fleming had never attended college, but he had challenged the Kansas Bar and was admitted on examination. Both attorneys were court-appointed and paid $10.00 per day.

By the late afternoon of March 22, the twelve jurors were seated and ready to hear the case. They were all local men and would be charged with both determining guilt or innocence and deciding what punishment would be meted out. The ones chosen were: Pete Merrill, a farmer; Otto Bader, a well water driller; Claude Harkness, a farmer; William Turrentine, a farmer; Albert Shackleford, Jr., a gas pipeline worker; Ralph McClung, a pharmacist; Dean Hart, a refining company salesmen; Jacob Dechant, a farmer; Ray Shearmire, a bowling alley manager; William Lewis, a nursery manager; N.L.Dunnan, an airport manager; and W. P. Bryant, a farmer. Each of them would be paid $5.00 per day and seven cents per mile for driving to and from the courthouse.

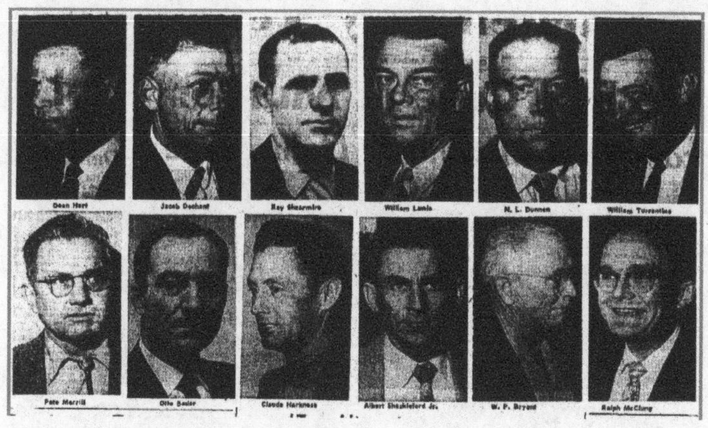

The Jury

In the gallery, Walter Hickock, father of Richard Hickock, was heard to say he thought that the process of selecting the 12-person jury had transpired very quickly. Many had expected it to take at least two or three days.

Also among the spectators were Herbert Clutter's brother Albert and his wife. As he walked out, he told a reporter for the Garden City Telegram that he came because he wanted to see the two men who had murdered the members of his family. He went on to say, "My attitude on this thing is awfully bad and I could tear them both apart."

Awaited by so many, this had long been publicized by newspapers across Kansas as "The Clutter Mass Murder Trial", and now - finally - it was about to begin.

Chapter 2

On the morning of March 23, 1960, there was a brisk wind blowing out of the north. The weather in Garden City had been the coldest recorded in March since 1898. That day would begin early for many. The sun had barely risen before the county courthouse was abuzz with activity. A line of Kansas State Police cars flanked both sides of the large old building. It seemed that each person moved with a certain urgency. As mid-morning approached, it was noted that a smaller number of spectators had arrived than for the first session. Many may have felt that they would be turned away once the seating space was filled to capacity.

The courtroom was located on the third floor. Additional wooden benches had been brought out of storage to help accommodate the expected overflow of curious attendees. Janitor Louis Mendoza had taken great pride in helping to prepare for the big trial. The spectator chairs and wooden pews, along with Judge Tate's bench and chair, were all hand-polished to a high sheen. They would be in the spotlight as the historic proceedings got underway.

Now that the jury had been selected and the defense and the prosecution were both ready for trial, the attendees and the world were about to hear all the grisly details of what Richard Hickock and Perry Smith were accused of doing inside the Clutter family farmhouse in the early hours of November 15, 1959. The Garden City Telegram's lead reporter, Bob Greer, would be in the front row and document it all in stark detail.

The Clutter murder trial dominated the headlines in all of Kansas's major newspapers. On the opening day, it would share the front page of The Salina Journal with the news that Great Britain's newest royal baby, born on February 9, would be named Prince Andrew.

Covering the proceedings for the Associated Press out of Topeka was Elon Terrance. Much of what America learned about the trial came from him. For the Kansas City Star, Dick Parr was on the front row. The Hutchinson News, The Topeka Daily Capital, and The Topeka State Journal also had reporters present.

At 9:40 a.m., Bailiff Leonard Smith called the court to order, instructing all in attendance to rise as the judge made his entrance. Judge Tate walked slowly from his chamber and climbed two steps to his seat at the bench. The "Be seated" command was issued, and the most historic murder trial in Kansas history had begun.

Next to enter the courtroom was defendant Richard Hickock. The 28-year-old was handcuffed once again to Deputy Sheriff Wendle Meier. Mere seconds later, defendant Perry Smith, 31, arrived - handcuffed to Deputy Sheriff Micky Hawkins. Both men were dressed in the same clothes they had worn at the prior day's hearing.

Then the jury filed in. They were all in casual attire. One wore dungaree pants with a western-style button-up shirt open at the collar. Few wore neck ties.

It was time once again for Judge Tate to outline for all present the rules he expected to be observed in his courtroom. That having been done, Court Recorder Lillian Valenzuela nodded to the judge that she was ready.

First to rise was County Attorney Duane West, and he detailed the four counts of first-degree murder that had been filed against both defendants on January 8, 1960. The two accused men showed little to no emotion as the charges were read aloud. Perry Smith sat motionless, staring straight ahead. Richard Hickock, nervously chewing gum, looked briefly toward the jury box. In the gallery, people listened intently to every word.

Continuing his remarks, West said, "Gentleman, the State of Kansas will prove to you beyond any doubt that Richard Hickock and Perry Smith are both guilty of these four murders, and we are prepared to bring to you a star witness who will tell you just how and when this plot was hatched to rob and murder the Clutter family." His words drew an audible gasp from the gallery, and people began whispering to one another.

Gripping a pencil hard, Perry Smith appeared uneasy. Richard Hickock, with his lips tightly closed and eyes shifting from side-to-side, tried to show no reaction.

There were more surprises to come. Without the foreknowledge of either the court or the defense attorney, West requested that Judge Tate allow all twelve jurors, court personnel, and the lawyers to board a Garden City school bus and travel to view the scene of the robbery and murders inside the Clutter Family farmhouse just outside of the town of Holcomb. The defendants would be transported by Kansas State Police vehicles.

The defense objected, saying the Clutter home had been changed since the murders occurred and seeing it would be of no value at that point in time. But Judge Tate overruled the objection and instructed the jurors to ready themselves for the trip to Holcomb. He then asked both defendants if they agreed to join those making the journey. Hickock and Smith glanced at each other, and it was Hickock who shook his head "no" first. Perry Smith, in almost a whisper, also rejected the idea. Court was adjourned by the judge at 10:23 a.m.

The morning was cloudy and damp as the jury members slowly made their way out of the courthouse to the waiting bus. Judge Tate stood by the door as the twelve men climbed the steps and seated themselves in pairs. He had issued strict instructions that no questions could be asked, there was to be no discussion among themselves, and cameras and recording devices were strictly forbidden. Twenty to thirty curious bystanders stood and watched, transfixed by the spectacle of a bus that normally carried the town's children to and from school now being used at a high-profile murder trial.

The ride to Holcomb was slow and quiet, allowing each juror to ponder silently what he might see and feel at the scene. The judge was transported in a Kansas State Highway Patrol car, and the attorneys drove their own vehicles.

As the bus finally made a left onto Holcomb's Main Street, only a few people were on the sidewalks. A southbound train passing through the town brought the convoy to a stop at the railroad tracks. Continuing on to the far southwestern edge of town, they came to Oak Avenue, where they took a sharp right turn down a long dirt road lined with Chinese elm trees. At the end was #611 – the Clutter home.

As they slowly left the bus, the jurors stood for a moment and gazed at the main residence and the large farm buildings that had once been the pride of Herman Clutter and his family. The expansive property was now empty, with no signs of human activity. A weather van atop the main barn turned gently in the wind, and the noise of crows could be heard in the distant fields.

They would be allowed to walk through all the rooms in the house. As the group moved forward, ominous dark clouds began to gather overhead, accompanied by thunder. The faces of some appeared somber and even sad.

And under their feet was what remained of the once immaculate front lawn, damaged by the crowd of over five thousand people who had attended the auction of the farm on the day before the trial began.

It had run from morning into the late evening. Before long, the mostly quiet and reserved group had swelled to such numbers that the Kansas Highway Patrol was called in to help with traffic control. Many were there because they wanted to see where the murders had taken place. Many came just out of respect. Kenneth M. Lyon, the administrator of the Clutter family estate, was in charge.

A lot of the farm equipment and personal belongings were bought by local farmers and families from around Garden City, Holcomb and other Kansas towns. The house and over a thousand acres of prime farmland were leased to Robert Harley, a farmer and rancher from Vinita, Oklahoma. Herbert Clutter had been in the certified seed grass business for the last twelve years of his life, and Harley had worked with him. He was liked and respected by the family and would use the land for the same purpose.

The last item to be auctioned off was daughter Nancy Mae Clutter's beloved horse "Babe". She had worked in the fields in her early years and helped the farm become prosperous and successful. Now, purchased by a local farmer for $182.50, she would spend her remaining years at the local YMCA helping the staff train young children to ride.

Each entrance to the Clutter house was now posted with a "Private Property – No Trespassing" sign. On the night of the murders, the killers had come through the side door that led into Herb Clutter's private office. It had been left unlocked. Today, the jurors and attorneys would follow in their footsteps in an effort to develop a better understanding of what had transpired.

One by one, they climbed the two steps and walked inside. The room that had once bustled with activity involved in managing a thousand-acre farm now sat eerily silent. It was small and gray in color. Few furnishings remained. One small picture on the wall hung at an odd angle. There wasn't space for the entire group to stop and look around, so they kept moving.

The wood floor creaked as they filed through the office on their way to the living room. From there, they could see the front lawn and surrounding fields through a picture window and contemplate the large white brick fireplace where ashes remained from those days when the house was still full of life.

It was in the kitchen that they first encountered evidence that something was amiss. Viewing the green telephone attached to the wall, they could easily see that the wire had been cut. Soon, the magnitude of the crime would start to come into focus.

A rush of musty-smelling stagnant air filled their nostrils when the door to the basement was opened. Most if not all surely knew in that moment that they were about to visit a spot where victims were discovered. Slowly, they descended the wooden staircase.

The basement was constructed of cinder block walls with a cement floor and divided into two distinct areas. One was designed for family recreation, and the other was a traditional utility room that held the furnace and water heater. Pipes ran along the exposed wooden floorboards.

Herbert Clutter's body had been in the utility room, and Kenyon Neal Clutter was killed in the basement as well. Now, the small, cramped space fell quiet as the members of the jury stood and stared, lost in their own thoughts.

And then it was time to go upstairs.

On the second floor, they viewed the rooms where the two female victims - Bonnie Mae Clutter and her daughter Nancy Mae - were found dead in their beds that November morning. As in most of the rest of the house, there was almost nothing left there to see after the auction had take place. With no traces left of the horrific slaughter, it was hard for them to picture what had taken place.

The group filed out of the Clutter home and back onto the bus for the return trip to Garden City. Several jury members could be seen turning in their seats to take one last look as they pulled away.

The ride back was quiet and solemn, with all of them taking time to process the day's events, perhaps even more aware now of their responsibility to make sure that justice was done.

CHAPTER 3

The afternoon session was called to order at 1:09 p.m. Prosecution attorney Duane West spoke first, setting the stage for what was going to happen in the courtroom. It was his intent, he explained, to prove on behalf of the State of Kansas beyond any doubt that the defendants Richard Hickock and Perry Smith had conspired to rob and murder the Clutter family.

As he was beginning to detail how Hickock had hatched the whole plot from his prison jail cell in the Kansas State Penitentiary in Lansing, a commotion in the spectator gallery diverted everyone's attention. Scuffling had broken out between county sheriffs and someone seated in the press corps section.

A small man with thinning light-colored hair, wearing a wool topcoat with a fur-lined collar, was being removed and taken out to the hallway. In a high-pitched voice, he protested loudly, "I am Truman Capote from the New Yorker magazine in New York. What is this all about?"

Truman Capote

Deputy Sheriff Wendle Miere searched his pockets and a shoulder bag. "I demand to know what this is all about," Capote continued. "I've never been treated as such!"

"You're being searched for a camera that we were tipped off to by a local reporter. Cameras are not allowed in the courtroom," Miere replied.

The search turned up nothing, and Capote was allowed to return to his seat in the reporters' section of the gallery. He could then be heard asking loudly, "I wonder who snitched me out to the cops?"

West continued his opening remarks, telling the court that a man with whom Richard Hickock had shared Cell #429 at the State Penitentiary in Lansing had worked years earlier as a farmhand for Herbert Clutter and had become aware of a safe in the home that he came to believe held as much as $10,000 in cash.

As he made his presentation, he stared intently at Hickock, who shifted from side to side in his hard-backed chair, chewing his gum nervously as he heard for the first time just what the prosecution had learned. And the spectators were silent as they remained focused upon on his every word.

Perry Smith was listening, too. He stared straight ahead, showing no reaction. But he surely knew that the noose for both of them had just tightened a bit more.

Now West stated his intention to put on the witness stand a man who could hold the key to unraveling the entire burglary and murder plot. Rumors had circulated through the news media that an informant had come forward with critical information that could break the case wide open. But the mystery witness had not been named in public or in the district court.

In the spectators' gallery, on the second row, Richard Hickock's father appeared worn out and weathered. Now, hearing about the surprise witness, Walter Hickock of Edgerton, Kansas, felt the full weight of the burden and sat with his shoulders hunched forward. He'd stood by his son all along, telling news reporters that despite a few brushes with the law in the past, Richard was a good boy growing up. He had kids of his own, the father said, and was incapable of committing murder.

The courtroom was restless with anticipation. Sitting behind the prosecution desk in the front row were Special Agents Roy Church, Harold Nye, Alvin Dewey, and Clarence Duntz of the Kansas Bureau of Investigation. That organization consisted of 19 special investigators who were all headquartered in Topeka. When a major crime was committed anywhere in the State, they would be called in to find the truth and solve the case. And these four were the best of the best.

Roy Church was the first to be called to testify. He was sworn in and took his seat with a look of total confidence. Duane West began by asking him to recount just what Richard Hickock had told him on that late afternoon of January 2, 1960, at the Las Vegas city jail.

Starting from the beginning, he reminded the court that Hickock and Smith had been arrested by the Las Vegas Police Department (LVPD) in the early evening of December 30, 1959, after being advised by his agency to be on the lookout for the two ex-cons, who were wanted for questioning and possibly traveling in a stolen vehicle.

While on routine patrol, LVPD officers Ocie Pigford and Francis Macauley had spotted a 1956 Chevrolet with out-of-state license plates parked in the parking lot of the Las Vegas Post Office. On a hunch, they ran a check on plate JO16212, and the results showed the car as having been stolen in Johnson County.

As they were getting that report from their dispatcher, a short, dark-haired man with a noticeable limp came out of the Post Office carrying a pine box and entered the car. He backed out of the parking space and began to leave. Pigford and Macauley followed cautiously, staying several car lengths behind the suspect vehicle.

The officers watched the driver head down Stuart Avenue to Main Street and then turn left, stopping opposite the Victoria Hotel on Bridger Avenue. At that point, they pulled in front of the Chevrolet and exited their vehicle with guns drawn, ordering the occupants to get out.

Richard Hickock and Perry Smith had been found and were placed under arrest on a Las Vegas sidewalk. The wooden box they had picked up at the post office was confiscated. One of the most intense manhunts in Kansas history had come to an end.

"It was late in the afternoon," Church continued, "by the time we got to Hickock." They had him brought to the interrogation room by Lieutenant B. J. Handlon, Chief of the Las Vegas detectives. It was a small space, with just a two-person desk and a couple of plain wooden chairs.

The two agents had begun by asking only about the bad checks Hickock had passed, the 1956 Chevrolet with Iowa license plates, and their travels around the United States and into Mexico. Church testified that the defendant, possibly relieved, was ready to take full responsibility for all of that, admit to having used bad judgment, and pay the penalty for his actions. He further promised never to write worthless checks again and to be a good, law-abiding citizen.

At that point, Church had looked down at his watch. The time was 5:30 p.m., he recalled, when he leaned back in his chair and asked, "Richard, where were you on the night of November 15, 1959? We're very interested in talking with you about the Clutter murders in Holcomb."

Shocked by this turn of events, Hickock had quickly risen to his feet and begun to protest, saying, "Oh, now wait a minute. I've had a few fights in my life but I wouldn't even kill a dog." Then he sat back down, noticeably nervous, and asked Agent Church for a cigarette. Church lit it with his Zippo. Hickock took a long draw on the Pall Mall and finally said, "Man, we did not have nothing to do with that." At that point, the interrogation ended, and he was taken back to his cell.

Church went on to describe the second conversation he had with Hickock, this one in the early morning hours of January 3, 1960, in the company of Special Agent Harold Nye. They returned to the subject of the back checks, with Nye suggesting that they clear that matter up once and for all and move on.

That prompted Hickock to describe each one he had written since being released on parole from the Kansas State Penitentiary on August 13, 1959. When he had finished, he tried once again to keep that as the focus of the discussion, admitting his guilt and swearing never to do it again as long as he lived.

But the agents were now ready to tighten the screws.

They sat for a few minutes, just looking at Hickock. Growing more and more uncomfortable, he buried his hands in his pockets and then took them out, stood up and paced a few steps, and then appeared to be trying to look through the mirror on the door, which was actually one-way glass.

Finally, Church spoke. "Richard," he said calmly, "We want to talk to you more about your connection to the Clutter family murders. We have information that you're connected to the four murders." At that point, Hickock broke. Returning to his chair, he nervously blurted out, "Look, I won't sign a statement and I won't testify in court, but Perry Smith killed all four of the Clutters. I did not kill anybody."

"Man, look," he continued. "When he started shooting, it scared the hell out of me. I thought he would kill me next. Man, his eyeballs looked like marbles poking out. He was, like, crazy. I did not know he was going to do it." Agent Church asked Hickock if he could draw a diagram of the house, labeling the rooms that the Clutters were murdered in.

On a piece of yellow legal paper, Richard Hickock sketched a crude layout of the crime scene. "Will you sign this for us?" Nye asked him. Hickock agreed to do so, saying, "I might as well sign it, but I am telling you the honest truth I didn't shoot any of those people and I didn't know Perry was going to shoot them."

As the session ended and Hickock was returned to his cell, the two agents were left shocked by what they had just heard. Lighting a cigarette and leaning back in his chair, Church gave a big wink toward Agent Nye. They sat there quietly for a while, taking time to relish the moment.

CHAPTER 4

The next person to take the stand was KBI Special Agent Al Dewey. He was a veteran of law enforcement and no stranger to the courtroom. The spectators were primed and ready to hear his testimony. No one said a word as he was sworn in and seated.

County Attorney West began in a loud voice, saying, "Gentlemen of the jury, Agent Dewey is now going to tell you just what the defendant Perry Smith told him on the morning of January 3, 1960, in the Las Vegas City Jail concerning the night of November 15, 1959, and just what really happened that night to the four members of the Clutter family."

"It is disturbing and it is gruesome," he warned them, "and you will never forget it. But it must be told."

Sitting straight in the witness chair and looking toward the twelve-man jury box, Agent Dewey started to recount what had happened.

In the very beginning, Smith had denied any involvement in the murders. But after being informed that Richard "Dick" Hickock had spilled the whole story and had implicated him as the one who killed all four of the Clutters, Smith began to talk.

Sitting in that small police station office in Las Vegas, leaning forward with both elbows on the small table, he was feeling betrayed and disgusted that Dick would turn on him. And he seemed to be relieved that their long run was over.

The agent testified that Perry told him it was Hickock who had set the whole thing up, planning it all from his prison cell at the State Penitentiary. Showing almost no shame or emotion, he asked, "Mr. Dewey, do you want to hear what really happened that night?" Raising his head slowly and staring straight into Dewey's eyes, Perry stated in a calm voice, "I killed Mr. Clutter and the boy, and Dick killed the mother and daughter." "And that is the truth," he continued.

"Right before we went in the house that night, Dick says to me 'Perry, we're going in there like a bunch of gangbusters.' Moments before we entered the house, Dick says 'Just look at this layout here. This guy is loaded.' We walked right in the side entrance door. It was not locked. It was on the west side of the house. It looked like a small office. We had a flashlight."

"Dick kept saying 'Look around. Check the walls for that safe. That damn safe is in here somewhere.' We went through each of the rooms downstairs, but we never found a safe. Finally, Dick says 'Let's get the old man up and he'll show us.' We entered a downstairs bedroom and there was Herb Clutter sleeping."

"The old man thought we were his wife. He said 'What is it, honey?' Then he realized it was not his wife and asked us what we wanted. 'Where is your safe at?' Dick asked him several times. 'Safe? What safe? I have no safe in the house,' Herb Clutter told us.

At this point Dick was getting upset and raised his voice, asking again for him to show us the safe *now*. Claiming over and over there was no safe in the house, Herb Clutter offered to write us a check."

"'We don't want a damn check!' Dick hollered. Standing in the kitchen area, Dick sees a wall phone and cuts the phone line. At this point, we both hustled Herb Clutter upstairs and woke his wife and we found his daughter and son sleeping. We got them all up and put them all in the bathroom together. After we put them in the bathroom, Dick went to every room checking for that safe. It just was not there. I remember telling Dick 'So this is your big score - a cinch.'"

"Looking through Herb Clutter's wallet, I think we found three ten-dollar bills and four five-dollar bills. When we went in the daughter's room, we found four silver dollars in a small cup inside a dresser. I found a radio and some binoculars in the boy's room. We took the money and stuff back downstairs. That's when Dick says 'Look, we're not leaving no witnesses behind.'"

"I followed Dick back up the stairs to the bathroom and we took each of them to different rooms. We tied up the mother and daughter in each of their beds. While we were tying up the young girl, Dick says 'She sure looks good. I might have to get me some of that.' I grabbed him by the throat, telling him 'If you lay a finger on that girl, I will beat the hell out of you right here.'

We took the old man and the boy down to the basement. We tied them both up. I remember the boy saying his neck was hurt. I looked around and found a small pillow and put it under his head. He was on a small sofa. That is when it all happened. Looking around that small basement, Dick says 'Come on; let's do it. We are not leaving no witnesses.' The basement was totally dark but for our flashlight beam."

"We first went to Mr. Clutter. He was thrashing around but tied tight and his mouth was taped. He was trying to say something, and Dick put the flashlight right on his head. I walked right up to him and told him I was just tightening the rope, and he never seen the knife. I came up from behind and cut his throat hard. He got one hand free and was trying to get at his throat. I grabbed the shotgun. Dick had the light right on his head. I aimed into the light and I pulled the trigger. The flash was like a blue white that lit up the whole room. Things moved fast now. We charged to the boy, and with the light on the boy's head I aimed and pulled the trigger again."

"We picked up the spent cartridges and ran for the steps leading out of the basement. As we ran up the stairway, we could hear the mother crying and in a muffled voice saying over and over 'Oh, no...oh, no.' We went to her first. It was at that moment that I handed the shotgun to Dick and said 'I cannot do any more.' He handed me the flashlight, and I put the light on the mother's head. She was begging 'Oh, please don't!' and Dick fired the shotgun."

"Only steps out of there was the young girl's room. I looked hard at Dick and flashed the light beam to her head. We had not taped her mouth. She begged us in those few seconds we stood there not to kill her. Finally, turning her head facing the wall with the flashlight right on her head, Dick aims and pulls the trigger. And it was all over."

"We rushed back down the stairs and Dick says 'Let's get the hell out of here.' We ran out of that house through the same door we had come in through. We left so fast we did not even shut the door."

As Agent Dewey finished recounting what Perry Smith confessed had happened that November night at the Clutter home, the court room sat in stunned silence. It was clear on the faces of all who had witnessed the testimony that none would ever forget the terrifying final moments the Clutter family had suffered at the hands of the two killers.

In the front row was Eunice Hickock, who sat with her head bowed in shame. At times, she appeared to be shaking as she heard the terrifying details of what her son Richard had been accused of doing.

As the court adjourned for its midday recess, word spread quickly of the gruesome nature of the crimes described by the agents that morning in Garden City. Many grew angry and wanted to see the ultimate punishment imposed for these senseless, horrific killings. In their minds, that meant seeing the two murderers swing from the gallows at Lansing. Amid the growing tension, Hickock and Smith were hurried back to their courthouse jail cells.

Most in the spectators' gallery didn't leave their seats, fearing if they even got up to stretch their legs someone else would quickly replace them. There was no shortage of people eager to hear firsthand the grisly details that were emerging on the witness stand. Many in attendance realized that they were witnessing what would surely become the most infamous murder trial in Kansas history.

At the same time, life in the town, for the most part, carried on as usual. On the evening of March 24, 1960, local families turned out in large numbers at the Clifford Hope Auditorium to watch the sophomore class of Garden City High School perform two one-act plays: "Don't Darken My Door" and "The Pest Guest".

CHAPTER 5

Judge Tate called the court back into session at 1:09 p.m. First to take the witness stand was Dr. Robert Fenton, the highly respected Finney County Coroner. Dressed in a gray suit and black wingtip shoes, he was there to describe being called to the murder scene and the condition in which he had found the four Clutter family members that early November morning.

"Nothing seemed to be out of order in the house as I walked through," Dr. Fenton began. "I did notice the wall telephone line had been cut into." Going first to the upstairs bedroom of Nancy Clutter, he had observed that she was lying on her bed facing the wall with both hands tied behind her back and then to her ankles and her feet were also tied together. She was clothed in a bathrobe, pajamas, and bobby socks and slippers. The shotgun blast appeared to have been fired at close range from the right, entering over her ear and exiting over her eye. The adjacent wall was covered in blood and brain matter.

Then, he had entered the room of Bonnie Clutter. She was found lying on her back, facing upward, with her hands tied together in the front. Her feet had been tied to each other and then to the bed frame. She was wearing a bathrobe and pajamas. She also had been shot at close range, with the blast entering her left temple and exiting the other side.

Next, Dr. Fenton testified, he moved to the basement. There, in a small furnace room, was the body of Herb Clutter, clothed in a striped bathrobe, pajamas and slippers. His hands appeared to have been tied but one was free and in an outstretched position. With his feet also tied, he had been hung from a water pipe attached to the floorboards of the ceiling. There was clear indication that his throat had been cut and his windpipe was severed, but his jugular vein had only been nicked. He was clothed in a striped bathrobe, pajamas and slippers. The gunshot entry wound was above and to the front of his left ear and continued through to the right ear.

On a sofa in another basement room, the Doctor found Kenyon Clutter in blue jeans, a white t-shirt and barefoot, with his hands and feet bound together behind his back. He had been shot in the face at close range, with entry just to the right of his nose and an exit wound at the back of his head.

In his professional opinion, Doctor Fenton said, all four victims had died instantly from their head wounds. By this time, people seated in the courtroom were visibly shaken by his testimony. But as the defendants sat listening, they showed little to no emotion or reaction. Shifting from side to side in his chair, Perry Smith seemed to be the more affected of the two and did appear to be uneasy.

Duane West called for Garden City Police Investigator Richard Rohleder to be sworn in as the prosecution's next witness. He was the official who had been tasked with bringing camera equipment to the farmhouse and taking 17 photos inside and outside before the victims were moved. They included three of Kenyan Clutter and two each of the other three victims. Rohleder told the court that he had photographed a bloody shoe print left on the cardboard that Herb Clutter was lying on and a second one on the concrete basement floor.

At that, Hickock's attorney Harrison Smith sprang to his feet and in a loud, firm voice objected to the photos being shown to the members of the jury, saying that they would prejudice and influence them. His objection was immediately overruled by Judge Tate. Meanwhile, Arthur Fleming flipped through the pictures, with Perry Smith sitting at his side. His client never batted an eye.

Each of the twelve men looked at the photographs and passed them on. No one spoke, but a look of disgust could be seen on many of the faces and several jurors could be seen shaking their heads. Shocking though they were, the 17 graphic pictures taken by Richard Rohleder that day also preserved for history the sordid details of the bloodbath that took the lives of the Clutter family.

Entered into evidence next were Exhibits 20, 21, 22 and 23. Contained in four separate clear plastic bags, they were the blood-stained ropes used to tie up the victims and the tape pieces used to cover their mouths. Then came Exhibit 25 – the blood-stained print of a right shoe heel, cut away from the cardboard on which Herb Clutter had been found lying. And that was the one that would draw the most interest. It clearly showed the iconic "Cat's Paw" logo found on a shoe repair product made by Boston's Foster Rubber Company and sold in the 1950s. That particular non-slip heel had become very popular, attaining almost a cult status. It's believed that famed pilot

Amelia Earhart was wearing "Cat's Paw" heels on a pair of leather loafers when she disappeared over the Pacific Ocean on July 2, 1937.

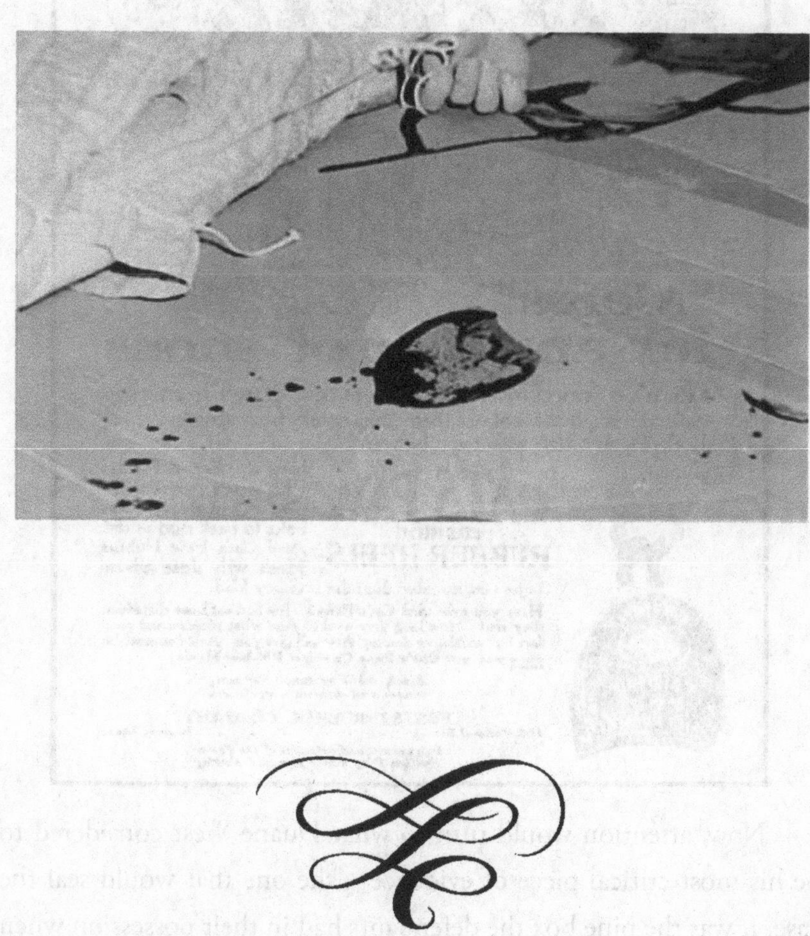

Now, attention would turn to what Duane West considered to be his most critical piece of evidence – the one that would seal the case. It was the pine box the defendants had in their possession when they were caught, and it was now resting on the prosecution's table. Moving outside the bounds of normal procedure, he asked that five FBI Special Agents step forward and be sworn in all at once by Court Clerk Mae Purdy. They were all from the agency's Crime Laboratory in Washington, D. C.

Agent R. Rena Bitez was the first of them to take the stand. A veteran of thirteen years with the FBI, he had spent the last ten specializing in blood and bodily fluids. When asked by County Attorney Logan Green to describe his experience, Bitez said that he had conducted tens of thousands of experiments and testified many times in State and Federal courts. Then, in a moment that would stand out as one of the trial's most dramatic, Green walked toward the box and stood for a moment with his hands in his pockets.

Reaching inside, he pulled out a pair of what appeared to be child-size black leather boots. First holding the weathered and worn items up, he suddenly dropped them on the table surface, creating a loud "thud" sound that startled many in the gallery. Over at the defense side, Perry Smith turned his head and studied the boots with great intensity. Attorney Green then asked that they be admitted as evidence. His request was granted.

Approaching the witness stand, he asked Agent Bitez to describe to the jury what his findings were regarding the blood found on the boots and the blood pattern on the cardboard section retrieved from the Clutter basement. He explained that each of the four victims' blood samples had been tested and that three of the victims had type O blood and one - Herb Clutter - had type A. The blood found under the right boot was a positive match for type A and so was the blood on the cardboard. Holding the boot high for all to see, Agent Bitez pointed to the heel section as being specifically where they had taken the sample.

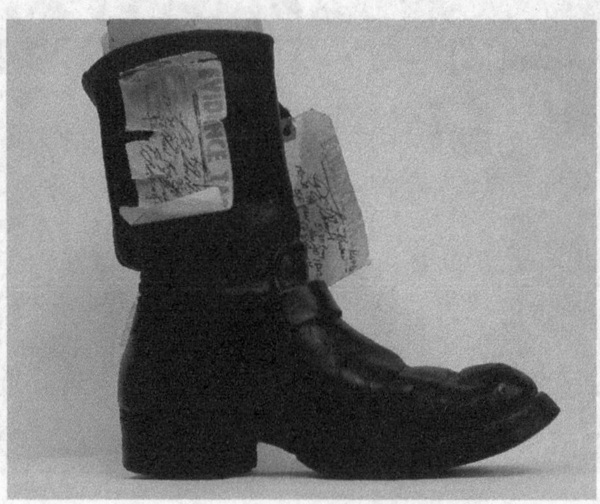

Returning to the box, Green reached inside again and removed an eight-inch, black-handled hunter's knife and requested permission to enter it into evidence. That having been accomplished, he handed the knife to Bitez and asked what his findings were regarding the item. The Agent replied that on first viewing, no stains of any kind were detected on either the blade or the handle. But once the knife was taken apart, six small blood spots were found in the handle section. All of them tested as being Type A.

His portion of the testimony completed, Agent Bitez was allowed to leave the witness stand. The prosecution then called Nancy Ewalt and Susan Kidwell, two teenage friends of Nancy Mae Clutter who had come by on that fateful Sunday morning to take her to church. They had discovered her body in the upstairs bedroom.

Nancy Ewalt would tell the court that her father, Clarence Ewalt, had driven them to the Clutter home.

"My father waited in the car," Nancy said, as she and Susan knocked on the farmhouse door. No one answered and the two, finding the door unlocked, opened it and went inside. The house was ghostly quiet, she remembered. Calling out several times with no response, the two girls bounded up the stairs leading to Nancy Clutter's bedroom. Almost instantly, they discovered the gruesome scene. Overwhelmed with shock, they ran screaming back downstairs.

Nancy Ewalt described the wall nearest the bed as being covered in blood spatter, and as she bolted from the room she had seen the victim's purse lying open on the floor next to a closet door. She continued her testimony, saying, "We ran from the house to my father. My father ran to the house and found Nancy Clutter's body and the body of Bonnie Clutter. My father tried to call for help from the house, but the phone line had been cut."

Surprisingly, both young girls managed to remain composed as they told of the horror they had discovered that morning. Many in the spectator gallery of the courtroom could be seen leaning forward in an attempt to catch every word spoken by their, soft quiet voices. At the conclusion of their time on the stand, they were escorted out by several Kansas State Police officers.

In total, eight witnesses would take the stand to relate their personal accounts of what they had seen that cold November morning.

CHAPTER 6

Late in the afternoon on March 24, 1960, there was a bitter chill in the outside air, and dark clouds and rain had moved over Garden City. Looking up from the sidewalk toward the fourth-floor, observers could see the yellow glow of the lights in the District courtroom. Many who could not gain entrance and had been turned away now stood mostly in silence with umbrellas open and overcoats pulled up high, waiting, watching and listening for some word of what had transpired during the trial.

Now, the prosecution team would finally call the surprise witness they had promised to introduce. And it would be these dozen or more people on the sidewalk who would get the first look at him. As a four-car Kansas State Police caravan pulled up to the old courthouse, most were caught by surprise, but many rushed the vehicles to get a closer close look at this mysterious individual whom so many had waited to see and hear.

There were two officers in each of the first two cars. The third held two officers plus one Sheriff and a single passenger. After disembarking, the group of no-nonsense Kansas lawmen formed a circle of protection around Scott County Sheriff Bob Brittan and the mystery witness. Walking briskly through the rain, the group entered the building.

The much-anticipated event was about to take place, and it was arguably the most dramatic moment of the entire process. County Attorney Duane West, stood, turned and faced the spectator gallery. In a loud, firm voice, he announced, "The State of Kansas would like to call to the witness stand William Floyd Wells."

At that very moment, the large old wooden double doors that led into the courtroom opened wide and, with Sheriff Bob Brittan by his side, the witness entered and walked directly to the front. Remaining on his feet only long enough to be sworn in with his right hand on the Bible, he took his seat. The hushed spectator gallery watched as Richard Hickock turned in his chair and aimed a cold, glaring stare directly at him.

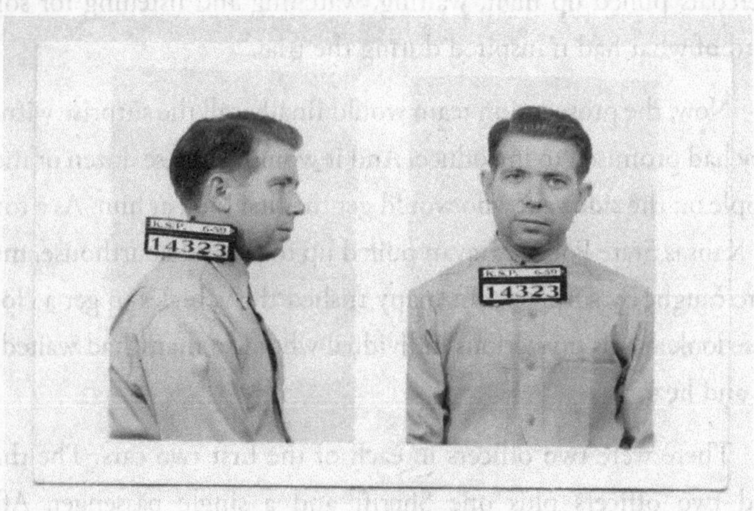

William Floyd Wells

Born in Oswego, Kansas, Wells was a 32-year-old high school dropout who had enlisted in the U. S. Army in 1946 and was honorable discharged two years later with the rank of Private First Class. Dressed on this day in a blue suit with a pale blue shirt and a dark blue tie, he folded both hands on his lap and leaned back in his chair. "Are you a resident of Kansas," asked County Attorney West, "and if so where do you live?" In an remarkably soft and low voice, Wells confirmed that he was a Kansas resident and was living at the State Penitentiary in Lansing.

Next, he was asked if he knew a man by the name of Richard Hickock - and if he did, to please point him out for the court. Without hesitation, Wells pointed directly at the defendant and said, "That's Richard Hickock". The two men stared silently at each other, and in that moment the tension could be felt throughout the court room. Then, West asked the same question regarding Perry Smith. Shaking his head, Wells denied knowing anyone by that name or ever meeting anyone named Perry Smith in his life.

Sitting at the defense table, Smith nervously flipped a pencil and glared over at Hickock.

The witness went on to say that he had met Richard Hickock in June of 1959 and that they were cellmates for at least 45 days at the Kansas State Penitentiary. He told the court that on one occasion, as the two men laid on their bunks in cell #429, he had mentioned that he worked for a Holcomb farming family by the name of Clutter in 1948 and 1949. He said he told Hickock that Herb Clutter was a nice man to work for and was always giving the hired farm hands a bonus in their pay and offering advances when they needed them.

Wells said, "I told Hickock that Mr. Clutter had told me once that he spends upward of $10,000 a week running his farm. I think I must have mentioned that I thought he must have had a safe up in that house. It was after I had told Hickock about that $10,000 that he just would not stop asking more and more questions about the Clutters. I guess it was about a week after I had first mentioned the Clutter Farm when Hickock one evening told me he was working on a plan when he got paroled."

"He said he had this friend named Perry Smith who would help him and that they were going down there to Holcomb and that Clutter farm and robbing them folks, and to be sure they would not leave any witnesses behind they would blow hair all over them walls. But that was the last we talked about it, so I just passed it off as big talk from another con and even before Hickock left on parole he told me he was going straight. He wanted to head west - maybe Las Vegas - and get him an Army Officer's uniform and pass bad checks and live the good life and even get him a boat."

"And then he was gone, so I didn't think anything more about him until one day when I was listening to my transistor radio in my prison cell, and I hear about this family murdered in Holcomb. A farming family. Then I hear it's the Clutter family. Then it really scared me. I just knew that Hickock had followed up on what he had told me he was going to do. He and Perry Smith were going to murder that Clutter family and rob them. He must have done it."

Wells stepped down from the witness stand and was ushered by Sheriff Brittan out to the waiting Kansas State Police caravan. Soon he was on his way back to Lansing. For his assistance, state prisoner

William Floyd Wells received a $1,000 reward and was granted early release on parole. And presentation of the prosecution's case had been concluded.

Now it was the defense team's chance to save both Hickock and Smith from possibly receiving the death penalty. They planned to call a total of five witnesses to the stand. The first of those was Walter Hickock, father of the defendant.

The elder Hickock stated that on the fatal night when the Clutter murders occurred, his son had told him that he and his friend Perry Smith were going to Fort Scott. He went on to say that Richard had returned home by supper time the following day and exhibited no unusual actions or emotion that might indicate that anything was any different from before. In fact, he lay on the couch and fell asleep watching TV.

Hickock's father went on to describe his early years, including how he had excelled at high school football, basketball and softball. "My son wanted to go to college, but we just couldn't afford to send him," he said. Glancing toward the jury box, he told of a serious accident his son had experienced in 1950. It was raining heavily all day, and he sent Richard out in the car to pick up some auto parts. Driving on Highway 56 from Olathe, he'd approached a school bus, lost control and flipped the car into a muddy ditch.

A man named Harold Rankin was first on the scene and tried to get Richard free of the wrecked vehicle. But Hickock had kicked like a wild animal. His head had been crushed, and Rankin could see that he'd sustained a severe head injury.

"It was after the wreck that we noticed a change in his personality," his father said. "We never knew what caused it, but Richard began gambling and hanging around older men and staying out all night and ended up arrested for breaking into a pharmacy. Later, we would find out that an older man had talked Richard into breaking into the pharmacy to help get money for his pregnant wife. Those charges were later dropped."

As the older Hickok ended his time on the witness stand and walked back to his seat, it was easy to see the toll that years of disappointment and stress had taken on him as he tried to stand by his son through it all.

Walter Hickock

CHAPTER 7

While doing the research for this book, we found recorded memories of several individuals who knew the young Richard Hickock and recounted examples of his well-known propensity for thievery early in life. Born on June 6, 1931, in Kansas City, Richard had a troubled youth that followed him everywhere. The Hickock family moved from Kansas City to Olathe in his early teenage years, hoping to start fresh. But they would find themselves embroiled in one bad situation after another due to their son's fondness for taking what was not his.

By 1945, they had packed up again and gone to Edgerton, Kansas, in an effort to give Richard another opportunity to straighten up and stop the constant stealing. But soon, things in and around that town as well started going missing. Purses would be stolen, and anything else left unattended was likely to disappear.

On one occasion at Edgerton High School, the principal called Johnson County Sheriff George Able to report that her pocketbook had been taken and Richard Hickock and the school janitor were sitting in her office at that moment. Sheriff Able recalled that Richard had initially denied having anything to do with the theft, but after a thorough search the pocketbook was discovered stashed in the school's boiler room and he confessed to taking it and hiding it there. The principle didn't seek to press charges.

As months passed and more and more things in Edgerton had been disappearing, suspicion began to mount that Richard Hickock was behind the wave of thievery. It had gotten so bad that in effect he had stolen everything in town he could get his hands on. The townspeople had initially thought of him as a kind and well-mannered teenager, but it wasn't long before they came to realize what a slick-talking con man he also was. The owner of the local gas station sold rifle ammunition from his station, and he said Richard would come in and buy several cartons of ammunition and then go across the street to an open field and shoot them as fast he could pull the trigger.

On another occasion, a Hickock family friend said that every time Richard stopped by his family's house to visit his children something would be missing after he left. Once, the man had put a five-dollar bill in a drawer as a bait to see if Richard would take it. Sure enough, when he checked it was gone. He called the father to report what had been going on. Walter Hickock pleaded with him not to press charges, promising to pay back the money and discipline his son.

The Hickocks had raised horses on their small farm. Finally, Richard had stolen so much and from so many Edgerton residents that the senior Hickock, trying to make amends for his son's actions, started giving a horse to each person who had been victimized. One of the townspeople said that you could always tell when Richard had stolen again. All you had to do was drive by the Hickock farm, and if another horse was gone from the pasture, you knew Walter had to pay someone off.

The defense called their second witness – Dr. W. Mitchell Jones, Jr., a psychiatrist from Larned State Hospital. He had graduated from the University of Texas School of Medicine and then interned at Detroit Receiving Hospital. Dr. Jones testified that he had performed psychological evaluations of over 1500 patients and assisted with the investigations of 25 murders. Having worked with both defendants, he stated that in his professional opinion Richard Hickock did know right from wrong on the night the killings took place. But he could not come to the the same conclusion regarding Perry Smith.

After the doctor's testimony had ended, both defense attorneys attempted to introduce the subject of the automobile and motorcycle accidents that had left both young men with permanent physical damage. This information quickly sparked an objection by the prosecution and was disallowed by Judge Tate as irrelevant. Attempts to bring several character witnesses to the stand were also blocked on the grounds that such material had no bearing upon the charges for which Hickock and Smith were being tried.

The trial had reached a critical point at which all of the damning evidence had been presented and the confessions of both men were on the record. Their last hope now lay with their attorneys' efforts to sway the jurors to show mercy and sentence them both to life in prison instead of recommending the death penalty.

Harrison Smith, Hickock's lawyer, stood and walked slowly to the jury box. With both hands resting on the railing, he said simply,

"Capital punishment has been a miserable failure, and criminality still abounds." Now pacing back and forth, he stated, "Capital punishment is for the poor – not for the rich." Taking a position in front of the jurors, he stood with his hands in his suit coat pockets and made eye contact with each of them. Smith continued to build his argument, saying, "Gentlemen, we do not want Richard Hickock released. We want him permanently isolated. Put Richard Hickock in a jail cell at the State Penitentiary in Lansing and throw away the key."

Hushed whispers could be heard from the gallery. Turning toward the spectators, Smith raised his voice and intoned, "Capital punishment is wrong! The law states that killing is wrong and then turns right around and kills. I ask this court - I ask you the jury - to spare the life of Richard Hickock and sentence him to life in prison. This whole tragic event is the result of a mixed-up mind. There is not one single act in this whole tragedy that is not from a mixed-up mind."

Walking over to the defense table, where Hickock sat with his head bowed, attorney Smith placed his hand on the defendant's shoulder and in a slow, even tone implored, "I am pleading with you for the life of Richard Hickock and pleading for the future when hatred will not control the hearts of men." With this dramatic close, the defense attorney had taken sixty-three minutes to make the plea on his client's behalf.

Now it was Arthur Fleming's turn. He described to the jury Perry Smith's early life, when he grew up in a broken home that was filled with struggle and pain and heartache. The family was constantly on the move, and both parents were abusive alcoholics. Finally, the marriage broke apart, and the defendant had lived at a series of institutions where he had been abused both physically and psychologically.

Standing only feet from the jury box, Fleming concluded Smith's defense by saying, "Gentleman of the jury, Perry Smith is a terrible damaged individual and we ask that you show mercy on him and sentence him to life in prison." At that point, hushed voices could be heard in the spectator gallery, and many of those in attendance could be seen shaking their heads.

Finally it was time for the closing statements. County Attorney Duane West rose from his chair and began his summation.

"The evidence in the case is overwhelming," he emphasized to the jury. The prosecution had bloody boot prints, the shotgun shell casings, the tape, the cord, the shotgun and the knife, and the confessions from both defendants. West walked to the evidence table, reached into the box and pulled out Perry Smith's right boot. "They washed the blood of Herb Clutter off the bottom of this boot," he stated. Turning and pointing a finger directly at Smith, he asked the jurors, "Can there be any doubt that this man is guilty of this horrible crime?"

Next, the attorney removed one of the shotgun shells from the box. Looking directly at Richard Hickock, he said, "This is the shell casing that Hickock scurried around to pick up after they had blasted Nancy Clutter to eternity. Gentlemen of the jury, please remember what Perry Smith in his confession told of those horrifying last moments the and pleas from Nancy Clutter saying, 'Oh, please don't!" and of her mother's last plea, 'Oh no! Oh, no!'"

"Most all of you in this courtroom, if you're from the state of Kansas, you know all about what we call 'that horrible western Kansas dust'. Well, for once we thank God for that dust, because in that dust was left the print of Perry Smith's boot covered in blood next to the body of Herb Clutter, found with his throat cut and shot in the head. What terror and horror those four innocent members of the Clutter family endured that morning. Regardless of who pulled the trigger on Richard Hickock's shotgun in this slaughter, both defendants are guilty of this horrific crime."

With that, West ended his portion of the presentation and County Attorney Green took over. Looking directly at the jury, he said, "Now it is your duty. Do your duty and do what you know is right." Leaning back and stretching out his arm for emphasis, he continued. "We don't want any chicken-livered jury members here who are out to let cold-blooded murderers off too easily. I want you to think about this. Poor Mrs. Clutter laying there in her own bed, hog-tied, and hearing her family members shot with a shotgun one at a time. Think about young Kenyan Clutter – all the years he had ahead of him."

Staring directly at the defendants, he finished his remarks with, "They tied the whole family up like a bunch of pigs and cold bloodedly murdered each of them. These two men went to the Clutter home to murder them and rob them. My mission is through. I have accepted my responsibility. It is now your duty to accept yours."

The State of Kansas had rested its case. And Richard Hickock shifted nervously in his chair.

It had been a long day. In the courtroom, local spectators and representatives of news organizations from around the country were anxious for a verdict. But Judge Roland H. Tate of the 32nd Judicial District was presiding over the most sensational trial of his career. When the time came for him to address the jury, he would do so at his own deliberate pace. It would take a full 45 minutes.

Only minutes, into the jury instructions, Richard Hickock's mother Eunice, seated in the front row of the spectator's gallery, burst into tears and had to be escorted out. Judge Tate reminded the attendees that order would be maintained in the courtroom.

There were 35 rules that the jury would have follow. It was stressed to the members once again that both of the defendants were presumed to be innocent until proven guilty beyond a reasonable doubt. As the prosecutor had told them, it would now be their responsibility to take the place of the blindfolded statue of justice.

Hickock and Smith had stared with no visible emotion and chewed gum while waiting to hear their fate. Now, as the jury filed out of the courtroom to begin their deliberations, they rose from their chairs and were walked back to the stairway that led to the jail on the top floor.

CHAPTER 8

Exactly one hour and thirty minutes had passed since the jury left the courtroom. It was 4:40 p.m. when the Foreman, W. P. Bryant, summoned Bailiff Leonard Smith. It seemed that the long-awaited moment of justice had arrived.

On hearing the news, spectators scrambled to return to the courtroom. Judge Tate was at his home feeding his horses when he was summoned by a Kansas State Patrolman to return because a verdict had been reached. Tensions reached a fever pitch in and around the building.

Perry Smith was brought in first, followed by Richard Hickock. Both were handcuffed and flanked by three Sheriff's deputies. The capacity crowd sat in silence as the 12 male jurors entered, walked in single file past the defense table and took their seats.

The booming voice of the bailiff instructed, "All rise!" Then the judge made his entrance and proceeded to the bench. Both Smith and Hickock once again were chewing gum, this time faster and with their eyes darting from one juror's face to another.

It was the first time during the proceedings that either of them had displayed signs of nervousness. Clearly, the reality of their situation was coming into focus. Were they doomed or would their lives be spared? After the lengthy nationwide manhunt, weeks and weeks of trial preparations, and then the actual trial, it had come down to this: the words that would be spoken in the next few minutes.

Judge Tate asked the foreman if the jury had reached a verdict. The answer was yes. As if in slow motion, the bailiff retrieved a slip of paper from Mr. Bryant and carried it to the judge. He took a moment to review the contents. Then, to a totally silent courtroom, he began to read aloud. There were eight counts in total – four against each defendant. On all of them, the verdict was the same: guilty of murder in the first degree. And the recommended punishment was death.

After confirming with the individual jurors that these were in fact their verdicts, he thanked them for having performed such a courageous service and released them from any further obligation.

And so, with those final words from the presiding judge, the trial officially ended.

The members of the jury were escorted out a side door, and the two now-convicted killers were marched back to their cells. In a moment of bravado captured for posterity by photographer Darrell Morrow of the Garden City Telegram, Smith and Hickock smirked and laughed for a moment before being separated.

The Kansas State Police, who had guarded entrances to the courtroom, now opened the doors to allow those who had just witnessed history out into the streets, and newsmen rushed for telephones to announce the verdict the whole nation had awaited.

By the time the word reached most citizens of Holcomb, the sun had set long ago, dark clouds had moved in, and the smell of rain was in the air. The streets were all empty, and for the most part only the sounds of the wind and horn blasts from a far-off passing train could be heard. A single light shone above Hartman's Cafe. Anyone peering through the small front window would see Bess Hartman hard at work cleaning the bar while waiting for the phone to ring. And the call finally came: "Both guilty on all eight counts of first-degree murder and sentenced to death on the gallows in Lansing." In a sense, it wasn't really official in town until Bess heard the news.

The verdicts and the sentences brought welcome relief and a sense of justice having been served. But the pain and sorrow and even some of the fear would endure. Life would go on, of course, in the small town. Not wanting to dwell upon grisly details of the crimes, most of the locals tried to avoid attracting the attention of curiosity-seekers who started coming to Holcomb from all over the country to see the Clutter house for themselves.

On the morning of April 4, 1960, the prisoners were returned to the courtroom, along with their attorneys. Richard Hickock wore a blue sport shirt and blue trousers and was handcuffed to Undersheriff Wendle Meier. Perry Smith, handcuffed to Deputy Mickey Hawkins, was dressed in jailhouse dungarees and a white t-shirt.

The court-appointed counsel for both men attempted to file motions that a new trial should be granted. They were quickly overruled, and their efforts were dismissed. It was then time for the jury's verdict to be approved. Asking the attorneys to stand, Judge Tate reminded them that under Kansas law he was required to pass sentence within five days. That was the cue for County Attorney West to make a formal request that the sentencing process be delayed no longer, and the judge agreed without hesitation.

He then looked at Richard Hickock and in a clear, firm voice said, "Step up here." Still shackled to Meier, Hickock stood and walked to within five feet of the jurist, glancing from side to side and nervously chewing gum.

"You have been tried and found guilty on four counts of first-degree murder," Tate intoned. "It is now the duty of this court to pass a formal sentence. Is there any reason that this court should not pass sentence on you?" he inquired. In a very low voice, Hickock answered, "No." The judge then asked, "Would you like to make a statement to the court?" Shaking his head slightly, Hickock responded, "No statement."

It was the moment of truth, and the fateful words were finally spoken: "This court rules that you, Richard Hickock, should be taken to the Kansas State Penitentiary in Lansing, and there you shall be hanged by the neck until dead on Friday, May 13th, 1960, at 12:01 a.m."

Now it was Perry Smith's turn. Instructed to step forward, he moved with a noticeable limp as he took the few short steps that would put him in front of Judge Tate. Glancing downward at first, he finally looked up and met the judge's gaze. "You, Perry Smith, have been found guilty of four counts of first degree murder, and this court will now formally sentence you," Tate said. "Do you have any statement you would like to make?" Again, the answer was "No."

"Is there any reason that this court should not pass sentence on you at this moment?" the judge continued. Speaking softly, Smith replied, "I can't think of any right now." All that remained was announcing the details, which were identical to those given to Hickock.

Next, Judge Tate instructed Clerk of Courts May Purdy to draw up death warrants for both men. They were to be be hand-delivered by Sheriff Earl Robinson to Warden Tracy Hand at the penitentiary and contained orders for him to receive Hickock and Smith and keep them safe until the date of their execution. Then came the final statement by the judge: "Mr. Sheriff, you may remove your prisoners from my courtroom."

The entire sentencing process had taken less than fifteen minutes to complete. Fewer than ten spectators had been on hand in the gallery. By late afternoon, the old courthouse was mostly empty. Attorneys and other personnel had gathered their belongings and left. Luis Mendoza, the janitor, was sweeping and cleaning up. He had been the one to bring in extra seats for the overflow crowd and polish all the old wood surfaces to a fine shine. Now, he would be the last one to leave.

Beginning the very next day, the focus would switch to the Kansas State Penitentiary, where both defendants would be taken - and where they would begin the long struggle to stave off their due punishment under the law.

Movement of Richard Hickock and Perry Smith from the Finney County Jail in Garden City took place shortly after 4:00 a.m. on April

5, 1960. Their last breakfast at the facility consisted of two eggs, toast and cereal. They had been incarcerated there for 90 days.

Unlike when they arrived that fateful night and found a waiting crowd of over 300, now there were no curious onlookers around to witness their departure. Secured with chains and handcuffs, the two condemned men had on their regular clothes, and Richard Hickock wore a black leather jacket. Perry Smith was heard to say, "Thank you for the courtesy you all have shown me" to the news photographers who had gathered to record the transfer, but Hickock remained silent.

CHAPTER 9

They made the 400-mile journey in separate cars, along with their individual warrants specifying the details of when and how the sentence of death was to be administered. The State of Kansas intended to ensure that neither of these two convicted murderers would ever kill again.

But in Garden City, opinion was divided. Many citizens felt that execution was entirely justified, given the heinous nature of the crimes. But others opposed the death penalty and thought that the legislature should enact new laws that banned its use. Can killers, if kept alive, be rehabilitated and someday function as upstanding citizens? Should we study them to learn how to prevent others from killing? Or, is it more important to protect society from the possibility that they'll kill again? It's an argument that still rages to this day.

Richard Hickock entered the prison first and was met by Acting Warden Sherman Course. Once both were inside, they were quickly moved to the small, red brick building that served as a reception area for new inmates. They were stripped and searched, and all of their personal property was confiscated. Hickock had 40 dollars in cash, his clothes and a few personal papers. Perry Smith turned over a small suitcase containing clothes, a fingernail clipper, a pen and pencil set and several family pictures. Both requested that the items taken be shipped to Hickock's mother in Edgerton, Kansas.

Within one hour of arrival, the two were in prison garb and occupying separate isolation cells in the maximum security section of the prison – the area better known as "death row". There was room for only six convicted murderers there, and the small, dank, dimly lit spaces were reserved for "the worst of the worst".

At that point, it seemed that their fate was sealed. But just days after being processed in, they heard some news that suddenly gave them some hope. Kansas Governor George Docking had commuted the death sentence handed down to 21-year-old Bobby Joe Spencer, convicted along with Gaither Eugene Crist of robbing and brutally murdering Mrs. Ruby S. Blanton, owner of a Kansas City rooming house. More importantly, the Governor indicated that he would take similar actions in any future cases involving capital punishment.

When specifically asked about Hickock and Smith, he expressed deep concern over how the rights of the two men had possibly been violated by sensational newspaper headlines such as "Clutter Killers Captured" before they had been found guilty in a court of law. He went on to say that the newspapers, in effect, tried the case in advance. Although they turned out to be correct in this instance, he felt that it set a dangerous precedent. The next time they might prejudice the jury pool against someone who was innocent.

On the morning of May 3, 1960, the Parsons Sun newspaper in Parsons, Kansas, reported that the $1000 reward offered by The Hutchinson News had been paid at the Kansas Industrial

Reformatory to inmate William Floyd Wells, Jr., for assistance that led to the arrest and conviction of Richard Hickock and Perry Smith. Three days after the reward was announced, Wells had revealed to the Kansas Bureau of Investigation the crucial information that broke the case. He was then moved from the penitentiary to the other facility.

The old Kansas State Penitentiary had been home to some of the state's most notorious criminals before Hickock and Smith were incarcerated there. Construction began in November of 1861, on a forty-acre parcel of land purchased from Almira Budlong for $600. The building and grounds were completed in 1864, built entirely by prison labor. John P. Mitchell was the first full-time warden, with Willem Dunlap, John Wilson and S. S Ludlan appointed to oversee the new facility. By 1875, the full-time guard force numbered 26 and the inmate population had reached 379.

Mitchell instituted the Silent System, prohibiting inmates from talking under any circumstances. But by 1881, the sheer size of the population created the need to keep them occupied. After a careful study, it was determined that a coal shaft could be dug and manned full-time by prisoners. That venture became so successful that it eventually supplied to coal to all of the State's institutions. The need to transport it became so great that the railroad relocated its tracks, a crossroads formed and soon the entire area around the prison was filled with new housing and businesses.

In only a short period of time, the fast-growing community had earned the designation "The Town of Progress". A subsequent industry – the manufacture of twine – was equally as successful, and both lasted until 1947, when they were discontinued due to high operating costs and reduced demand. The penitentiary had bought two thousand acres of land and began to grow crops and raise cattle, poultry and hogs. That farm operated until 1975.

The old stone walls of the prison made the small and primitive cells seem cold and damp and hard. Sounds echoing through the iron gates were a constant presence day and night. Frightening screams and cries and shadows around every corner created an eerie sensation that those who experienced it would never forget. Over the years, it was said by many that the old place had the look and feel of a medieval dungeon and the grave was all too often the only escape.

Those who survived their time behind bars were never the same again. The penitentiary was designed to administer punishment, and Richard Hickock and Perry Smith could expect it to be their last home until the day they swung from the prison gallows. They were considered to be extremely dangerous, and both were escape risks.

In his final days at the Finney County Jail, Hickock was moved to an isolation cell because a makeshift shank-type weapon was found under a mattress in the bullpen-type environment where he had initially been held. It was believed that he might have been planning to attempt an escape. The device was formed from a one-and-a-half-foot piece of wooden broom handle with a highly-sharpened piece of number 12 wire from a toilet bowl brush attached at the top. When confronted, Sheriff Robinson reported, Hickock denied ever having seen the weapon.

Following the the recommendation of the prison classification committee, Warden Hand had put the men in strict segregation under close custody. There were to be no job assignments for them or interactions with the general population. Hickock was inmate number 14746 and Perry Smith's number was 14747.

Receiving and sending mail was restricted for both. Hickock's list of exceptions included Walter D. Hickock, now in Garnett, Kansas, Paul Hefley and Leslie Roades of Kansas City, Kansas, Kirk Merrillatt and Eunice Hickock of Bethel, Kansas, Frances Boyd Oshel of Edgerton, Nelle Harper Lee of New York City and Truman Capote of Brooklyn Heights.

On Smith's list were Tex J. Smith of Golconda, Nevada, Nellie Harper Lee of New York City, New York, Dr. Mitchell Jones of Newton, Kansas, Truman Capote of Brooklyn Heights, and Wendy and Josephine Meier of Garden City, Kansas.

On the morning of April 11,1960, the attorneys for Richard Hickock and Perry Smith filed the first appeal to the Kansas Supreme Court asking that a new execution date be set while the two were awaiting the outcome of pending their appeal.

Sitting in their isolation cells, the two had little to do but ponder their fate. And then Smith succumbed to the pressure. On May 24, 1960, he was heard by death row guards telling Hickock, "You can wait around for the rope, but I'm going to beat it." At that point, he began a hunger strike and expressed his intent to starve himself to death. He refused to speak and turned away all food and liquids.

On September 4, 1960, the Manhattan Mercury newspaper reported that his actions had caused prison officials great concern. Guy Rexroad, Director of Penal Institutions, asked the Kansas Supreme Court to review the state of Smith's sanity, saying that his mental condition had deteriorated considerably. The high court rejected the request but did decree that the prison must take take care of Smith and, if need be, transfer him to a state hospital.

By mid-October, Smith had lost 59 pounds and weighed just 105. He still refusing to communicate in any way. Director Rexroad instructed the prison staff to continue to encourage Smith to eat and provided a mix of milk and eggs.

A month later, Smith had begun to consume small portions and was drinking a milkshake mix through a straw. He would speak a few words but was barely audible. The Garden City Telegram reported on November 15, 1960, that Smith had put a few pounds back on. Hickock, meanwhile, was eating regular meals three times a day and gaining weight.

CHAPTER 10

As both men's appeals slowly worked their way through the Kansas court system, Richard Hickock, in a surprise move, filed a legal notice with the Garden City Telegram and sent a copy of it to Finney County Attorney Duane West. It read, "I, Richard Eugene Hickock, sentenced April 4, 1960, for the crimes of murder four counts in the first degree in Finney County, Kansas, will apply on 12/29/60 for executive clemency to Governor George Docking at his office in Topeka, Kansas. Signed: Petitioner Richard Eugene Hickock."

The legality of such a move was by no means certain. West was quick to respond that usually the Governor's office is not asked to exercise clemency until all court actions concerning appeals have been completed. The clerk of the Kansas Supreme Court, Walter Neibarger, said the Supreme Court of Kansas would not hear the case until January, 1961, at the earliest or possibly as late as March. He also confirmed that neither Hickock nor Smith could seek executive clemency before the court's decision had been rendered.

Both condemned men held out hope that Governor Docking would consider commuting their death sentences to life in prison.

The death penalty in Kansas had been abolished in 1907 and remained controversial until it was restored in 1935. Then, no executions were carried out until 1944.

Since 1954, the Governor, a staunch opponent of capital punishment on moral grounds, had blocked them entirely. When pressed on the matter, he said, "I just don't like killing people." He failed to win a second term in 1960, and his commutation of the death sentences of Wilson and Spenser was widely blamed for his loss. At the end of the year, with Docking's replacement about to take office, there appeared to be little if any hope remaining for Hickock and Smith.

Kansas prison archives show that Perry Smith and Richard Hickock had filed for executive clemency from the Kansas Governor's office in July of 1960. Records Clerk Richard R. Barker processed the forms, and on July 28, the petitions were denied.

On December 29, the outgoing Governor released a statement through his pardon attorney, Dale Spiegel, making it official that his office would not recommend clemency for any capital murder cases still before the Kansas Supreme Court. Spiegel had conducted hearings in Topeka involving two of the four that were pending. As each was called, it was noted that Richard Hickock had no legal representation. By the Noon deadline, none had arrived.

On January 6, 1961, it was announced that the long-awaited appeals by Hickock and Smith to the Kansas Supreme Court would be heard on February 27. Duane West would present the case for the prosecution. West, of course, had represented the State in the 1960 murder trial and won the convictions of Richard Hickock and Perry

Smith. But in a strange twist, he had been defeated in his bid for re-election as Finney County Attorney by Harrison Smith, who had been appointed by the court to represent Richard Hickock during that same trial in Garden City. Now, Dale Corley was to take his place as legal counsel for the plaintiff during the appeal proceedings.

Perry Smith ended his eight-month-long hunger strike and was returned to death row from the prison hospital, where he had been receiving nutrition intravenously and through the nose. Warden Tracy Hand reported on February 1 that he believed Smith, now weighing just 104 pounds, had used the tactic as a ruse to obtain a transfer to the state mental hospital for the criminally insane in Larned. The staff had become convinced that he was not nearly as weakened as he pretended to be.

The tipping point was reached when Deputy Warden Sherman Crouse entered Smith's room and, finding it to be warm and stuffy, opened the window and turned on a small fan. Two hours later, he returned to find the fan off and the window closed. Perry Smith, who supposedly could barely move or speak, had been alone in the room the entire time. The incident was duly reported to the Warden, who issued instructions on January 30 for Smith to be issued a prison uniform and told to get dressed. He walked back to his cell on his own.

On July 10, 1961, the Kansas Supreme Court announced its long-awaited findings, ruling that Richard Hickock and Perry Smith had been properly convicted in their murder trial the previous year. No evidence could be found to support the contention that either Hickock or Smith was temporarily insane at the time of the murders.

The verdicts and sentenced handed down by the district court were thus upheld.

The high court's unanimous opinion was authored by Chief Justice Jay Parker. He wrote that the court, after reviewing the entire trial transcript as well as the abstracts of the representing parties, had failed to find any plain error, specified or not, that would justify or require reversal. In their motions for a new trial, attorneys for both Hickock and Smith had contended that they had not received a fair trial, primarily because the court had failed to appoint at least one psychiatrist to the commission of three physicians that had examined them.

The doctors determined, after a thorough examination, that Richard Hickock and Perry Smith were both sane and did know right from wrong at the time of the murders and therefore could stand trial. The Supreme Court ruling noted that a psychiatrist appearing on behalf of the defendants also testified that Richard Hickock knew right from wrong at the time of the murders but offered no such opinion on Perry Smith.

The defense had made the additional claim that the defendants did not receive a fair and impartial trial due to the overwhelming media coverage by local and state and national news outlets. In response, the high court wrote that after a close examination of the transcripts they could find no claim by either defendant that prior to or during the proceedings he was being deprived of a fair and impartial trial by the news media.

Following the ruling, Dale Courey and Arthur Fleming, attorneys for Hickock and Smith, announced that they would each be filing a rehearing petition with the state Supreme Court as required by law before a hearing could be appealed to a court at the federal level. At the same time, both stated that they would not be filing any further appeals for either of the convicted killers. If Hickock and Smith wished to continue the appeals process through the federal court system, they would need to hire new attorneys.

On the morning of July 28, 1961, the rehearing petitions were submitted to the Kansas Supreme Court with hope that it would agree to review its decision upholding the convictions and sentences. There was no indication of when that ruling might come, so at that point the two convicted men could only sit in their cells and wait – knowing that their very lives hung in the balance.

Life in the old penitentiary was anything but pretty or easy. There were two levels of security at Lansing: "I" for isolation and "S" for segregation. Segregation was for the hard cases – the men who for one reason or another could not associate with other inmates and weren't even granted whatever meager privileges the rest were allowed. Many who lived in segregation referred to it as "the hole".

Heavy metal screens kept the prisoners from throwing items out of their cells. They had no heating except for the large radiators in the main corridor. Heavy iron bars and cold, gray stone walls were everywhere. The foul smells were horrific. Inmates endured, on a daily basis, a nauseating blend of disinfectant, old scum in cracks and crevices, and the accumulated stench of men living in close quarters for years on end.

On the top floor, in the eastern most corner of the segregation building, a steep staircase led to a steel catwalk that ran past five cells.

It was the only way to access death row, home over the years to some of the state's most notorious murderers. Now, two of those ancient cells held Richard Hickock and Perry Smith.

On the outside, just past the heavy walls, stood an old, weathered warehouse with a dirt floor and a constant dampness in the air. Depressing as the environment was, pigeons had found it suitable and could always be seen nesting in the rafters. In a far corner, barely visible in the dark, was the gallows. Crudely constructed of heavy wood planks bolted together, with thirteen steps from the ground to the top, the massive structure had stood for decades in silence. In 1961, in Kansas, this was the designated instrument of legal execution.

Chapter 11

As the legal wheels of the Kansas justice system turned slowly, the State Supreme Court, acting upon the recommendation of the Kansas Bar Association's Legal Aid Committee, appointed Wichita attorney Russell Shultz on November 28, 1961, to represent both Hickock and Smith. He was directed to initiate any further proceedings necessary regarding constitutional questions arising from their murder trial in Garden City.

His first filing, on December 22, questioned whether there should have been a change of venue and also if the defendants had been properly represented by legal counsel. He further raised the possibility that Judge Roland Tate might have been friends with one of the murder victims.

The petition filed by Shultz requested that a commissioner be appointed to hear testimony and set out four grounds for a writ of *habeas corpus,* specifically:

(1) Hickock and Smith were convicted and sentenced to hang without due process of law;

(2) they were not properly represented by legal counsel;

(3) widespread and inflammatory publicity had highly prejudiced the inhabitants of Finney County so that they were not able to obtain a fair and impartial jury; and

(4) the men were denied separate trials.

The new year of 1962 would see a series of court filings serving to bolster Richard Hickock's and Perry Smith's hopes their death sentences might be overturned. On January 16, the Kansas Supreme Court appointed its former Chief Justice Walter G. Thiele as a commissioner to hear evidence and make suggestive findings of fact and conclusions of law concerning their cases.

Less than a month later, Attorney General William M. Ferguson designated Charles E. Vance as a special assistant to help defend against the *habeas corpus* writ, stating that "the Attorney General's office has made a thorough investigation of the trial and we are convinced beyond any doubt that both Hickock and Smith received a full and fair and impartial trial. Mr. Vance will assist the state in vigorously opposing any effort to set aside this conviction and sentence."

The hearing was set to begin on February 13 at 9 a.m. in the Finney County General District Courtroom in Garden City, site of the original trial.

Commissioner Thiele had issued twenty subpoenas to individuals he wished to appear. That number included all twelve sitting jurors, the two alternates, presiding judge Roland Tate, defense counsels Harrison Smith and Arthur M. Fleming, prosecutor Duane West, court reporter Lillian Valenzuela, and Bill Brown, editor of the Garden City Telegram. Neither Hickock nor Smith would attend, as the Attorney General's office had decided that the risk to the community of transporting them from Lansing would be too great.

Assistant Attorney General J. Richard Froth, representing the State, was quoted as saying that it would be up to attorney Shultz to prove his allegations. What had started as a rumor was now the subject of open discussion in Garden City: Shultz had taken the case only because he was being paid a large sum of money.

Incensed by that implication, he emphatically responded, "No, I have not been paid one cent. And as far as I know, all of my expenses will come out of my own pocket." He went on to explain that the Kansas Bar Association had supported his appointment to the case but had no funds to pay him. They had stepped in because Richard Hickock was a prolific letter writer and had corresponded with many groups around the country - some even communist in nature - to ask for their legal assistance. That prompted Everett Stearman, Chairman of the Legal Aid Committee, to look into the matter and then recommend him as counsel.

The hearing got underway at 9 a.m. on the appointed date. Former juror Bill Lewis was called to the witness stand first and was followed by Pete Merrill, Dean Hart, Otto Bader, Albert Shackelford, Jr., W. P. Bryant, Claude Harkness, William Turentine, Ralph McClung, Jacob Dechant, Ray Shearmire, N. L.Dunnan and then alternate jurors Larry Lobmeier and Ottis Jennings. Each was asked if he had any acquaintance with any member of the Clutter family before the murders took place and whether he had formed an opinion as to the guilt or innocence of Hickock or Smith prior to the trial.

Seven of the men testified that they were acquainted with Herb Clutter but had never interacted with him socially.

All twelve jurors testified that they were not social acquaintances of any of the Clutter family members, and none said he had made up his mind beforehand. Then, Shultz began to request that they reiterate their individual positions on capital punishment, as stated during the jury selection process. At that point, Judge Thiele interrupted, telling Shultz that he saw no purpose in that line of questioning.

The attorney stood and responded, "I have heard statements that one of the members of the jury when questioned answered, 'Normally I don't. But in this case, I do.'" Hearing that, the judge allowed Shultz to continue. And juror N.L, Dunnam confirmed that he had, in fact, said, "I do not usually favor capital punishment, but in a crime of this magnitude I do favor it."

As the proceedings moved on, Attorney Shultz told Judge Thiele that because of his investigation it was his feeling that due to the enormous publicity and the general animus of the community, a fair jury could not have been assembled from Finney County and a change of venue should have been granted. He called both defense attorneys to the stand to address that question.

Harrison Smith testified that he based his decision to allow the case to be tried in Garden City upon the fact that members of a local organized group called Ministerial Alliances that strongly opposed capital punishment had been speaking out publicly against hanging the two defendants. Asked if he had ever felt personally threatened in any way for representing his client, he produced a post card sent to him by an anonymous individual. On it was written that he would be a much more popular individual if he lost the case. For his part, Arthur Fleming had simply believed that people in that area would be more lenient than those in other parts of the state.

Next on the stand was the Garden City Telegram's long-time reporter Bob Greer. He was asked to identify a picture snapped by the paper's photographer, Darrell Morrow. It had been taken in the late evening of January 6, 1960, in front of the county courthouse, where a large number of local citizens were gathered to witness the arrival of Richard Hickock and Perry Smith after their arrest in Las Vegas. The crowd was estimated to be well over three hundred people. Greer testified that he had not witnessed any hostility and sensed instead more of a jovial atmosphere than anger or threatening behavior.

By day's end, the twenty witnesses had taken the stand and answered all questions from attorney Shultz. In essence, they told the court that no change of venue had been requested by either defendant or was thought to be necessary at the time of the trial. Further testimony confirmed that neither the members of the jury nor the presiding judge had been close friends with any of the Clutter family and that the court-appointed defense attorneys had performed their duties to the very best of their ability and had not done so reluctantly. And there had been no indication of a threat directed at either lawyer or any lynch-mob attitude toward the defendants upon their return to Garden City from Las Vegas after their capture.

As the proceedings moved toward a close, it was announced that on the following day the hearing would be continued in a room deep within the walls of the maximum- security Kansas State Penitentiary in Lansing, so that the two convicted prisoners could attend and testify.

CHAPTER 12

The next morning, shortly after 9 a.m., Richard Hickock was brought in with chains around his waist and connected to handcuffs. His legs were shackled as well, and a prison guard was stationed on each side. Perry Smith followed, similarly restrained. He moved awkwardly with a noticeable limp, and his face grimaced in pain. All eyes were on him as he struggled to get to his seat.

After swearing them both in, Judge Thiele began his questioning of Hickock. Dick Parr, longtime reporter for the Kansas City Star was there to record the event. Hickock related to the judge that he had spoken with his attorney, Harrison Smith, just three times before the trial. "I told Mr. Smith I wanted a change of venue," he said, "and he told me that it would not do any good because the feelings about the case were the same all over the state. I also told Mr. Smith I wanted a separate trial from Perry Smith, and Mr. Smith filed a motion for a separate trial and it was granted. And by the time we went to trial, we were tried together."

Hickock further testified that when he was brought to Garden City for arraignment he was met by a crowd of between 400 and 500 people and had overheard someone yell, "Look at them guys. Don't they look tough? We ought to take them out and hang them right now!" He also stated that the first time he met his court-appointed attorney he was told, "Looks like they're going to hang you, boy."

He continued, adopting somewhat more cocky tone, "I'll tell you this. I know for a fact that the *voir dire* examination of the jurors was not taken for the record. And I thought on appeal that would throw the case out in a hot minute." A *voir dire* examination is given to a prospective juror or witness and mandates that they tell the truth. It's also used to determine if the individual is rendered ineligible to serve by having a personal interest in the matter before the court. And attorney Shultz took the position that the trial court erred in this case when it failed to perform the *voir dire* examination as required.

Judge Thiele looked directly at Richard Hickock as he sat motionless at the defendants' table. It was clear that he had suffered permanent damage to his head from a severe automobile accident years earlier. His head appeared to be slightly lopsided and his eyes looked asymmetrical. Thiele asked the defendant, "How much education do you have?" Hickock responded that he was a high school graduate. In earlier testimony, he had told the court he waived his rights to a preliminary hearing without knowing what he was doing.

Learning forward with both elbows on the table, the judge inquired, "You mean you did not know what a preliminary hearing was, and yet when you testify you know what such legal terms as severance and separate trials and *voir dire* examination mean?"

With his eyes shifting from side-to-side, Hickock explained that while in prison awaiting his execution, he had been studying law. Without another word, Judge Thiele slammed the black wooden gavel down and called for a recess.

When the hearing resumed, Perry Smith was called to testify. Asked if he had ever heard the word "venue" before, he responded in the affirmative but said that he did not know what it meant. Smith, who had only a third-grade education, went on to say that his attorney Arthur Fleming had told him before the trial that he was in favor of the proceedings being held in Garden City and did not wish to ask the court for a change of venue to another county in Kansas because he was a former mayor and felt that fact might help with the case.

After Smith had completed his testimony, there were only two witnesses left to be called that day. The first was Mrs. Eunice Hickock, mother of Richard Hickock. Her appearance before the judge was relatively brief. She related that before the trial had begun, she had overheard attorney Harrison Smith tell her husband that the trial must be held in Garden City and that the defendant's father had subsequently died of cancer on June 28, 1960, in Edgerton.

She was followed by <u>Topeka State Journal</u> reporter Ron Kull. The journalist testified regarding a story he had written in which Harrison Smith was quoted as saying that there were citizens of Garden City who were hostile toward both Hickock and Smith prior to the trial.

At that point, Judge Thiele called a recess until February 19.

The *habeas corpus* hearing was drawing to a close. On the final day, Sheriff Wendle Meier, who had been undersheriff and jailer of Finney County at the time of the trial, was called to testify. He had escorted the two fugitives back from Las Vegas and estimated the size of the waiting crowd to have been 150 to 200 people. Contradicting Hickock's testimony, Meier described the group as "curious", saying "I think they just wanted to get a look at these boys." The only comment he heard by anyone came from a child, who said, "They sure don't look like no murderers to me."

He confirmed that defense counsels Harrison Smith and Arthur Fleming had both conferred with their clients prior to the trial, estimating the total number of meetings as being between 15 and 25.

That last bit of business having been completed, Judge Thiele issued instructions to the defense and the prosecution to provide their findings of proof no later than March 5th. He further set March 10th as his deadline for submitting his opinion to the Kansas Supreme Court.

Patience was wearing thin in Garden City. Locals had openly expressed their frustration and bewilderment that two men who had confessed to the horrific cold-blooded murder of four innocent victims could now be allowed to raise questions regarding whether or not they had been treated fairly under the law. Now, once again, there would be reason to hope and believe that the defendents' pleas had been in vain. Judge Walter Thiele formally recommended that the writ of *habeas corpus* be denied, writing that he had been unable to find a shred of evidence that the two had been denied a fair trial or due legal process.

The Kansas Supreme Court convened on Monday, June 4, 1962. Attorney Russell Shultz would have the task of making the final plea to the Justices on behalf of the defense. He opened by stating that his purpose for appearing was not to discuss the guilt or innocence of Hickock or Smith, whose actions on that fateful day in 1959 were undoubtedly horrible. Instead, he went on, the question up for consideration was whether their rights to a fair and impartial trial had been fully protected as guaranteed by the Constitution.

In short order, the final arguments had been made and the evidence was in the hands of the high court. And so the waiting game would begin anew.

Back on death row, Hickock and Smith rarely spoke to one another, though they were in adjacent cells. Years later, former guard Jerry Collins would say that he had gotten to know both men during the five years of their incarceration, having had many conversations with them. Never once had either shown any remorse for having committed the murders. "Always a con man," he said of Perry Smith. "He tried many times to con me. He was a smooth talker."

When the high court ruling came on on June 7, it was front page news all over the state. The Garden City Telegram wrote "Killers Fail in Move to Escape Death". In The Parson Sun, the headline was "Hickock and Smith Lose Again in New Trial Bid". The Lola Register reported in bold print "Clutter Killers Lose Plea", and The Ottawa Herald read "No New Trial for Clutter Murders." This final decision all but spelled the end of Hickock's and Smith's chances for reversal of their convictions by the Kansas court system.

Moments after the ruling was read, Russell Shultz addressed a throng of news reporters, expressing his disappointment and assuring them that he now intended to take the case to the United States Supreme Court. If refused a hearing there, he said, the defense team would present the issue to the Court of Appeals. They remained convinced that Hickock and Smith did not receive a fair trial and should have been granted a change of venue due to strong feelings regarding the case in Finney County, prejudice of the jury, and newspaper stories about the crimes.

The Kansas Supreme Court also announced that Richard Hickock and Perry Smith had become critical of attorney Shultz and his services and had asked that the court replace him with a Kansas

State Penitentiary inmate who had offered to represent the two condemned men. But the court ruled that only members of the Kansas Bar were permitted to represent clients before the Supreme Court, and so that request was denied.

Chapter 13

The appeals and motions for new trials having all but ended, it was now necessary to set a new execution date for the two men. If any appeals were going to be made at the federal level, the executions could be stayed while they were being heard. In a release dated September 10, 1962, the high court announced that the date was to be October 25th. The hangings were to take place between 12:01 a.m. and 4:00 a.m.

As the process dragged on through the legal system, many Kansans were disappointed in the slow pace. Some expressed their frustration in personal letters written to then-Governor John Anderson, Jr., and kept in his files. Here are some examples:

Dear Sir,

Two years ago now, ourselves and enough others voted Governor Dockings out of the Governor's office. Although he had been an average-to-good governor, but for the sole reason we wanted such men as the Clutter family murders given their punishment as sentenced them in a fair trial. We are not bloodthirsty people. But when men have confessed to such a brutal act, how can you be justified in spending the tax-payers money to defend them again? No one has any desire to have their crime reheard again. It was loathsome the first time. Besides, our money could be put in much better uses. I think I speak for the majority of Kansas citizens when I say – let justice be done so we can forget about the whole gruesome mess.

Most sincerely,

Mrs. Chester King

Dear Sir,

Could you tell me why the convicts that murdered the Clutter family near Garden City Kansas have not been sentenced after two years? I am frequently asked this question as I travel over Kansas and elsewhere. Some say lawyers delay cases to receive more money. I would appreciate an answer. Justice is certainly slow in this case.

Sincerely,

Cornis R. Reese

Dear Governor,

We are very much annoyed by constantly hearing the postponed execution and new trials for the killers of the whole four members of the house family at Garden City. What kind of laws have we set over our "great state"? How many of these murderous brutes have to kill to justify the extermination such demons of our society in Kansas? They admitted the murders, so why give them an excuse account lasting years? The fact that they did this horrible act is sufficient proof that such characters are a grave danger to society. And the sooner executed the safer for society. Who is irresponsible for this delay?

Yours truly,

A. C. Bergmann

Dear Sir,

As governor it is up to you to do something about this. Just what kind of laws do we have in our state, that murders can be allowed to kill a Kansas family (good citizens of the state) and not be punished? Just how many more years are they going to be allowed to live and then maybe set free? They should have been hung at sunrise as soon as they were found guilty. No wonder we have so much crime in our state they know they will never be punished. Just a housewife concerned for her state.

Evelyn Haynes

Dear Sir.

In the spirit of Christmas, I respectfully request you to commute the death sentences of Richard Hickock and Edward Smith to life in prison.

Respectfully,

Gordon D. Wiebe

As the wheels of Kansas justice moved slowly, so did the time spent on death row for both Hickock and Smith. There was very little to do but wait and wonder. Both men read and drew pictures, and Perry Smith even dabbled in painting. For Richard Hickock, writing letters would ease the loneliness of his isolation. Many of them have been saved. One that he wrote his to mother Eunice said:

"Dear Mom,

It is Tuesday evening and I decided to write you a few lines, so I will probably quit before long and finish tomorrow.

I had a visit today from a couple of preachers who drove up from Newton Kansas. They were Mindinites (however you spell it) and were the emotional insistent type. They seemed to be in their late sixties or early seventies and were a couple of dandies. I suppose the old gentleman meant well and I appreciate their interest, but I don't like forceful methods. They did not want to take no for an answer in my regard to my salvation. I know as much about the "bible" as they did.

I think they were both part time farmers. And the crying, loud talking, floor rolling kind. They asked me to get down on the floor. With as much diplomacy as I could muster, I declined there offer and remained in my chair. One started crying and waving his arms while shouting prayers. And the other started a foot stomping chant of "a men". I thought they were a couple of refugees from the house of David. They kept shouting that time was short and the second coming of Christ was appoun us.

A loud knock came at the door and I thought it was him, but it was only a colored boy getting a chair for the officer to sit on. I looked at the officer and he looked at me and I wondered if I could outrun him to the door. One of the men stopped long enough to ask me if I felt it. The only thing I felt was a headache coming on. I said to him "feel what" he looked at me like I had insulted him.

After about five minutes of this they got their handkerchiefs out and the next five minutes were spent cleaning their noses out. They started reading verses out of the bible and their voices were so loud that over hundred men in the yard lowered their heads. But being serious it was quite a sight. When they left both promised to come back. I told them to write first I wanted to be ready for the next session.

They were doing what they thought was right and that is the important thing. I do appreciate their thoughts and it shows that some people are considerate, even thou they are nuts. I exaggerated a little describing them, but you get the general idea. You might tell Carol about it she might get a kick out of it. I am drawing some pictures of you and Carol and the boys. As soon as I finish, I will see if I can mail them to you. All I have to use to copy from is the small snapshot's, plus I'm just starting so I hope you will take that into consideration when you see them.

I haven't received any additional news since I last wrote you, with the exception that I received permission to write Nations thru Mr. Corely in Garden City. Corely drew up the contract but he may not wish to handle such an arrangement. In the event he does not other arrangements can be arranged.

Well, I suppose I just as well close for now. I did not intend to write so much tonight, but I got carried away. Hope you are feeling

OK. Have you got your teeth yet? Did you say David's new address is RR 1 Wellsville, Kansas? I don't know if I am going to send him a Christmas card or not. I would like to mail him a baseball bat so he can use it on himself. He sure isn't doing you right. I can understand about me, but not you. He ought to be horse whipped, if Dad was alive, he would do it. Lots of love. Dick."

The two preachers that Hickock mentioned were The Reverend C.B. Friesen and Mr. E.J. Classen. Their visit had been arranged by Kansas State Penitentiary Chaplain James E. Post and approved by Warden Tracy Hand. Hand controlled all access to Richard Hickock and Perry Smith. He had set down strict rules: One-hour visits one time each month between Monday and Friday. No weekend or holiday visits. Only members of their immediate families were authorized. But as time passed, more and more other individuals from all over the State sought permission to visit the prisoners.

One of these who contacted the Warden was The Reverend Floyd Holland, founder of The World Bible Fellowship of Lyons, Kansas. In a lengthy letter , he asked to send scriptures and inquired about the possibility of a personal visit. He wrote, "Sir, I know they have done wrong. But even what they have done can still be forgiven by God, for the Lord said he is not willing that any should perish but that all should come to repentance. Please do not cast this letter away and disregard it, but I so want to help these boys. May we be granted this permission."

On April 19,1961, Warden Hand denied his request, reiterating that only immediate family members could see or correspond with death row inmates.

But if Holland would like to send religious literature to the Institution's main office, he said, the clerks would see to it that Hickock and Smith would receive it.

Chapter 14

In Richard Hickock's cramped #15 cell, he had stacked his books and drawing supplies very neatly in a row at the foot of his bunk. The books had all been selected and personally approved by Warden Hand. All his drawing supplies were individually searched before being given to Hickock. His small book collection included Tropic of Capricorn by Henry Miller, Fanny Hill by John Cleland, Lolita by Vladimir Nabokov, Here Goes The Kitten by Robert Gover, and The Snake, I The Jury, Vengeance Is Mine, and The Long Wait, all by Micky Spillane.

The Kansas State Penitentiary was a highly-organized state institution with strict rules and regulations. If an inmate needed even a pencil, he would be required to fill out a request form. For the men on death row, all requests would be granted or denied by the Warden. The "Inmate Request to Staff Member" form simply instructed inmates to "state completely but briefly the problem you desire assistance (be specific)" and included the date, the time, and the inmate's number and name.

Richard Hickock used the form many times during his stay. One of the more amusing requests was filed on September 7, 1960. It read

"To Mr. Hand Warden. Dear Sir. Would it be possible for the men on death row to get some water Mellon to eat? Thank you R.E. Hickock." In the reply section, the warden responded, "Other inmates who are confined to the S & I units do not get any watermelon so therefore your request is denied. Warden Hand." Another time, he asked to be allowed to purchase ice cream from the inmate's store along with his candy and cigarettes. Approval was granted, but only for Saturday afternoons at two p.m.

After months of enduring long hours of isolation, both Hickock and Smith were showing signs of growing weary and mentally depressed. Richard Hickock wrote this lengthy letter on September 12, 1963, to Robert J. Kaiser, Director of Kansas Penal Institutions in Topeka:

"Dear Mr. Keiser."

"I am writing this letter with a great deal of concern and apprehension; not entirely for myself, but with the mental physical welfare of others in mind. The circumstances for writing this letter are numerous; therefore, the letter in all probability will be quite lengthy. I ask your indulgence in reading it and that you give the contents your close attention. For such I will be truly grateful."

"First, to clarify my intentions I feel that I should point out that my position is one that is unstable to say the least and the nature of my incarceration is such as to cause my (also the other men on death row) opinions and views to be those that cannot coincide with the general run of prison inmates. I do not wish for this letter to be construed as criticism of any individual or the policies of this institution. I can't honestly feel I am in any position to criticize anyone."

"My sole intention in writing you am attempted to point out several causes for mental depression – depression of such magnitude, as to cause the contemplation of possible self-harm in order to gain temporary or permanent relief. I have been hesitant and reluctant in writing you, hoping that some form of relief would be administered, without the necessity of making a request. However, it is my belief that the officials of this institution are not fully aware or realize what a man daily is being forced to suffer, due to the lack of necessary facilities for the correct type of incarceration for men condemned to die. Only a man incarcerated over a lengthy period of time, under these same circumstances, can realize a full understanding of what truly exists."

"I shall attempt in my limited vocabulary to set down a comprehensible account of existing conditions with the hope that you will grasp the importance of the situation and grant the desired relief-indeed needed relief. A man sentenced to death - the ultimate punishment- has an entirely different and a somewhat distorted outlook on life. His mental condition is such as to render him intolerant, nervous, irritable, irrational, and depressed. Thus, adverse transpiring events cause nervous stress and strain, that would be tolerated by those of any other type of incarceration. Even a man on death row can stand most anything over a limited period of time."

"At the time of writing this letter I have been incarcerated a total of forty-two months. This entire time has been spent in solitary confinement. The only method available for men on death row to passing the long hours of each day is to read or draw. My first three years on death row were passed with reading only. This has led to almost exhaustion of the prison library (books fit for reading) and arriving at the mental state the mere thought of reading sickens me."

"The men on death row were granted the privilege to purchase art supplies – of a limited variety. Some six months ago now I purchased $50 in art supplies, pastels, crayon's, paper and have discovered that to pass my time at such an occupation is more expensive than I readily can afford. Also reading and drawing from the light shed from sixty-watt bulb twelve feet from the floor is eyesight destroying. I have been forced to quit both because of my weakened eyesight and the frequency of headaches. Therefore, my time is spent staring at the four walls and pacing the floor."

"During a cell shakedown a couple of weeks ago my drawing board (a sheet of cardboard) was taken and torn into strips. Consequently, I have nothing to draw on in the event I desired to do so. It was a waste of $50 which I cannot afford to waste. I purchased art supplies and now cannot be able to use them."

"The building here at the institution used for housing death row prisoners is a catch all, antiquated relic a century old. It is a disgrace before man and a shame before God, to incarcerated men in such a dungeon as this, that would do justice to the "Spanish Inquisition". Mental patients are housed here prior to their transfer to Larned. These men who cannot be blamed for their actions, scream, yell, pound on the walls, whistle and raise hell in general. Some of these men continue their Shann agons for as long as four to five days and nights. This means the men on the row can have no rest, no concentration on reading, writing, drawing and causes mental strain of terrific proportions. This is a punishment we are suffering that was not prescribed by law."

"The building houses those men who have violated rules and regulations. Men who are placed in isolation for punishment. These men consider their predicament as a joyous experience and the building a playhouse. They shout yell and joke and tell dirty stories all hours of the day and night. This also means a constant strain on the nerves, no concentration, no peace of mind and no regularity in living habits. This leads a man to contemplate the possibilities of self-destruction as a means of gaining a relief."

"Men are housed in this building who are on protective custody. Men who had no consideration for their fellow convicts while in the population and have no consideration for those incarcerated in the close confines of this building. These men will make a chess board numbering each square on the board. This enables them to shout numbers to men in other cells there by designating their moves and allows the playing of their game. These games sometimes are four games going all at once. They last for hours on end. Thereby setting up a nerve shattering roar of numbers that have the men on the row ready to commit mayhem in order to gain a short period of solitude. This leads to arguments, threats, and remarks in regard to what we are in here for. Other men express their hopes in regard to our end at the end of a rope. Such incarceration is not for animals much less men."

"I realize that the present physical plant here at the institution precludes any possibilities of segregating the men on death row. I realize also that a new S & I building is to be constructed. However, I as well as the men on death row will be long dead prior to the completion of any new building. So, the new S & I building will aid us not one iota. However, a remedy is now available, which I will discuss later."

"As I am writing this letter, I hear one man is screaming to send him a couple of song books three or four men are going to sing. Such infantile, childish, immature caterwauling you have never heard in your life. It is all I can do to keep what sanity that I still possess. If I or of the other men on death row would request the others to hold the noise down a little, they would immediately in no uncertain terms tell us what we could go and do to ourselves. This is what we have been suffering for over three years."

"It is now approximately ten o'clock at night, and I was forced to shut my window, the only source of ventilation in the cell. The reason for closing my window is the accumulation of hundreds of bugs around my light bulb which burns twenty-four hours a day (not only mine but everyone's light bulb in segregation). At night all thru the summer little green bugs start coming into the cells around nine o'clock. These bugs get in a man's hair, ears, eyes, nose, mouth and bite worse than a mosquito (the night officers on duty will testify to the truth of this). With the window closed the heat is unbearable. One is forced to pour water on himself. The privilege of having a fan was granted but no fan was ever given."

"I would like to insert at this time the fact that in my forty-two months of incarceration I have had no exercise. My entire time I have spent inside my cell. As are all men on death row. I realize and appreciate the fact that no exercise facilities are available. However, such conditions cause dire results both physical and mental. Without exercise a man has no appetite his food looks like so much garbage. I don't eat one third of it I throw most of it away. The food is good wholesome and well prepared. But I have no appetite (it's the same with all the men on the row)."

CHAPTER 15

"All the fore written conditions cannot be remedied. Not with the present physical plant. However, ninety percent of the mental strain and depression can be relieved. How? By allowing men on death row a radio with earphones. One radio placed in the hallway with attachments for four earphones would give the men a welcome relief from the mental turpitude prevalent in this type of incarceration. A man could put on the earphones and not have to listen to the childish idiotic pratterings of these other men. He could place himself mentally outside of these walls in a world of music, sports, house opera, and news events. Music is soothing to anyone's nerves. It keeps the mind off of one's troubles family, financial, death, etc. A radio is the answer to our mental depression."

"If a man was to be incarcerated under these conditions for a short time only, he could readily endure it or if it was to be a long incarceration the mere knowledge of eventual release would be enough to endure most anything. However, a man sentenced to death can glean no pacification from any future possibilities. Long endurement of such conditions destroys a mans will he needs most a will to live. Without this a man will seek death. A radio has been denied us in the past because of the fact that other men are in this building. These men are not on death row. They are not sentenced to the ultimate penalty. Almost all of them could get out if they made an honest effort and indeed, they all will eventually and not by dying. Just recently three men who had been in here excess of three years settled their differences and are now in the population. There is little chance if any for the men on death row to ever go to the population and have access to radios maybe TV movies athletics et sets."

"The other men in S & I can get out there. Most of them by asking. This is why I feel we are entitled at least to a radio with earphones. If necessary, we will provide the necessary funds for the purchase. I hope I have given some idea of the true situation here on death row. I know we are not here to enjoy ourselves, but nothing could be furnished that would bring this about. I do not believe anyone appraised of this situation and understanding its literal horrors would hesitate in granting this one request."

"Our penalty for what we have been convicted of is giving of our lives. I do not believe the law intended for a man to be forced to endure such mental turpitude to the extent of inflicting self-harm in us to gain relief. I'm not saying anyone will, but the possibility now exists and is bound to become more so through extended incarceration under present conditions. I sincerely plead that you will grant this privilege as soon as possible. Upon consideration please advise."

"Respectfully,
Richard Eugene Hickock"

Hickock wrote on behalf of the five death row inmates: Perry Edward Smith #14747, Lowell Lee Andrews #14606, James Douglas Lathom #14698, and George Ronald York #14699 and himself. But it would fall on deaf ears.

The response from the office of the director of Penal Institutions, Guy Rexroad, was addressed to Warden Tracy Hand. The warden was instructed to inform the inmates that their request for radio privileges for the death row section of the Segregation and Isolation building was denied. Rexroad pointed out that the inmates not on death row but in the segregation section of the building were not given access to a radio. The possibility of hooking up earphones on death row that could be connected to the prison's central radio station had been considered but quickly dismissed due to the absence of funds in the budget for such a purpose. Later, the warden would receive a direct request from Eunice Hickock that her son be allowed to have a transistor radio, which she would purchase.

It was February of 1963, and still the appeals were dragging on. The two condemned men were using every avenue possible to avoid their date with the hangman. Speaking to a group of lawmen in Garden City, Kansas Attorney General William Ferguson reported that they had asked for a writ of *certiorari,* which – if granted – would mean a review of both their original appeal to the Supreme Court and the *habeas corpus* action in the State court. He stated that he fully understood the frustrations of law enforcement and the public at large regarding the glacial pace of the process but reiterated that all persons are entitled to exercise whatever options are available to them under of the law.

On the 18th, the United States Supreme Court made its decision that there would be no review of the case of Richard Hickock. In May, it also denied Perry Smith's appeal. Shortly thereafter, the Attorney General's office in Topeka announced that it would now be up to the Kansas Supreme Court to set a new execution date.

As more and more citizens in Kansas and all over the West continued to express their concerns regarding the Garden City murders, editorials began to appear. In one, titled "Is The Crime Irrelevant?", a resident who had traveled to the northern part of the state recalled being asked, "When are you folks going to do something about those Clutter killers who are still alive?" He wrote in response, "It's a fair question, but the responsibility cannot be limited to those of us living here. The snail's pace of the wheels of justice is a concern to all citizens. Due process of law, the unalienable right of every citizen, has become synonymous with 'delayed process'."

"Although the appeals for a review of their case before the United States Supreme Court have been rejected, Richard Hickock and Perry Smith have not exhausted their avenues of delay. These two have admitted their guilt to the cold-blooded premeditated murder of four people. They have been judged sane at the time of their trial. The evidence against them proved guilt beyond a shadow of doubt. Yet they have delayed their punishment – death on the gallows – by appeals that they did not receive a fair trial."

"It was more than three years since a jury in Finney County rendered a verdict. The cry from this corner is not revenge. It isn't possible to even the score. But we do raise our voice to a system which permits what we view as 'going through the motions" to delay punishment without any legitimate basis with which to do so. Their right to appeal can't be denied, but there is no excuse for the long delays in the rulings."

In their editorial "The Mill Grinds Slowly", published on June 6, 1963, the Topeka Daily Capital wrote:

"The convicted murderers of the Herbert Clutter family of Holcomb have come almost to the end of the line. Richard Hickock and Perry Smith, ex-convicts, were convicted in Finney County District Court early in 1960 of one of the most heinous crimes ever committed in Kansas. Although their confessions to the slaying of a prominent farmer, and his wife, and two children were not admitted into court, Kansas Bureau of Investigation agents testified to the confessions and at no time has there ever been any question of the guilt of the pair. Through legal maneuvers, Hickock and Smith have been able to drag out their trial appeals for more than three years."

"The pair who slew four without mercy have had their appeals heard by the Kansas Supreme Court, both on appeal from the conviction and on an application of writ of *habeas corpus* when the Kansas Bar Association wanted to make certain that they had received a fair trial. Individually, Hickock and Smith have appealed to the Federal Courts and the United States Supreme Court. In each instance, decisions have been against them, as could be expected."

"Aside from the long delay, the state has been at considerable expense because of the appeals. Attorneys representing them have not only donated their time and effort but have been out of pocket for travel and other expenses. It can be hoped that it will soon come to an end which was seen when they were arrested in Las Vegas only a short time after the murders. Justice has moved too long with dragging feet."

And Whitley Austin, Editor of the Salina Journal, added his opinion on "The Cruelty Of Delay":

"Four years ago, next month, four members of a prominent farm family were brutally shot to death in their home in Holcomb in southwestern Kansas. For this murder, Richard Hickock and Perry Smith were arrested, tried and convicted and sentenced to death. Except for those who prohibit capital punishment 'under any circumstances', it was the consensus that society could protect itself against such men only by eliminating them. Their backgrounds, their prison records, the cold-blooded and unprovoked murder itself, all indicated they were an intolerable menace."

"Those that oppose the death penalty, however, argued that society is the real criminal in the case, that we have collectively failed in education and reform and that the slayings should be on all our consciences. In part this is true, although this does not mitigate the crime nor make the execution of the murderers less justified. Now we collectively have another matter on our consciences."

"After a series of appeals and hearings and technical arguments, the case of Hickock and Smith is still before the courts. Their guilt is not in question, but the technicalities of their convictions seem to be. Four years is a long time, unreasonably too long, cruelly too long for the course of law to take. Certainly, the pair deserve every chance of appeal, every protection of the law; no one asks for cottonwood justice. But to spin out the procedures until the case threatens to outlive evidence and witnesses, to delay the operation of the law is an outrage on justice."

"It is a manner of thwarting the law, reducing its effectiveness, of bringing discredit upon it. The various judges, lawyers and clerks and their suicidal habits of procrastination may be directly to blame. However, it should be on all our consciences that we permit the law to be mocked in this sad fashion."

On Wednesday, June 26, 1963, the Kansas Supreme Court made public the new execution date, instructing the Kansas State Penitentiary at Lancing to carry out the punishment on August 8 of that year between 12:01 and 4:00 a.m. But then, a new question was raised – one that would lead to yet another legal battle.

Hickock's home had been searched in January of 1959 by Kansas Bureau of Investigation agents Harold Docker and Wayne Owens.

The shotgun and hunting knife used in the murders were found and confiscated. However, the search had been carried out without a warrant. The defense attorneys felt that was a violation of their clients' civil rights and petitioned successfully for a hearing on that basis in the United States District Court in Topeka.

CHAPTER 16

Both Richard Hickock and Perry Smith were set to appear before Judge George Templar on October 9. Days before, Robert J. Kaiser, who was the Director of Kansas Prison Institutions, sent the judge a letter. In it, he vigorously argued against any move to have the prisoners confined in a city or county jail or to prolong their stay outside of the custodial facilities at the State Penitentiary at Lansing. He asked if the hearings could instead be held at the Leavenworth Federal Courtroom. If that could not be arranged, he suggested, perhaps both Hickock and Smith could be brought back to Lansing each night after the proceedings.

Director Kaiser reminded the judge that one of the convicted murderers had boasted that he would not die on the gallows. Due to the length of time since their sentencing, he feared, they could have become more desperate. He stated, "I certainly would not like to be responsible for any violence that maybe initiated by either of them. We consider that both men, if given the right opportunity, could be extremely violent. It is our hope that the court will be understanding concerning these particular prisoners."

In a separate letter, Warden S.H. Crouse expressed his concerns regarding the length of the hearing, considering the fact that at least thirty-one witnesses would be called. He felt that could lead to both Hickock and Smith being required to stay overnight in Topeka and outside of the penitentiary, a confinement situation that could create a serious security issue.

But these expressions of concern were set aside, and the hearing would begin as scheduled. Joseph P. Jenkins of the firm Cohen, Shneider, Shamberg & Jenkins had been appointed by the Court to represent Hickock, replacing Wichita attorney Russell Shultz. Shultz had been arraigned in the U. S. District Court in September, charged with failure to file federal income tax returns for 1958, 1959 and 1960. He eventually pled guilty to one of the charges, and the other two were dismissed. Shultz was fined $1000 and put on probation for one year.

Security was tight as the hearing began. All doors leading into the courtroom were guarded. Dressed in prison-issued blue serge double-breasted suits with white shirts and wearing leg shackles, Richard Hickock and Perry Smith sat at opposite ends of the defense table, under constant watch. Both had yellow legal pads and pencils to take notes if they chose to.

Attorney Jenkins sat beside Hickock, and Robert H. Bingham, representing Smith, was next to his client. The prisoners, showing the effect of their incarceration, exhibited a definite prison pallor. In the front row of the courtroom, Kansas City Star correspondent Robert H. Clark was prepared to record and report details of the historic process.

Richard Hickock's mother Eunice was the first person called to testify. Now gravely ill, she recounted that two Kansas Bureau of Investigation agents had come to the family home in Edgerton, Kansas, knocking on her door in late January of 1959. They identified themselves and requested permission to enter. "They asked to speak to Richard," she said, "and I informed them that Richard was not at home. They then asked had I seen a man named Perry Smith."

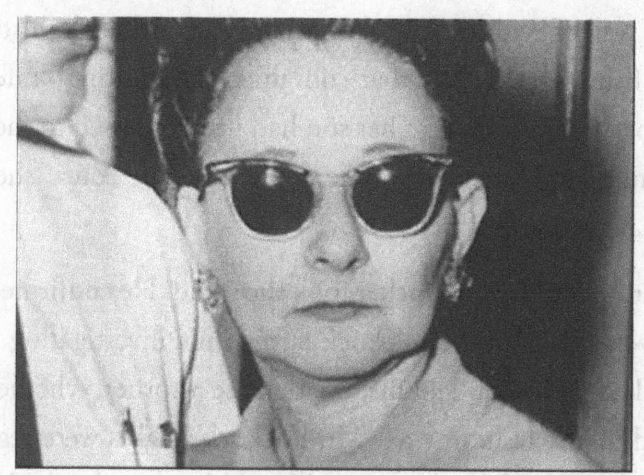

Eunice Hickock

She had informed the two agents that both her son and Perry Smith had left for Fort Scott, Kansas. Sitting in the main living room area of the house was a wood stove, and leaning against the wall behind the stove was a 12-gauge shotgun. The agents examined the gun but didn't take it with them when they left, Mrs. Hickock told the court.

"They searched our house and our barn," she continued. "At the time, I didn't object, and I didn't know about the legal requirements of a search warrant. They said nothing about my rights. I thought when an officer of the law asked you to do something you had to do it. But they did take a work uniform of Richard's and they took four shotgun shells from a carton they found in our cupboard."

Mrs. Hickock went on to testify that at around midnight on January 3, 1960, the same two agents returned to the Hickock farm and this time demanded both the shotgun and the hunting knife. "We've come for the gun," she recalled Agent Owens saying. She said that Walter Hickock, Richard's father gave the shotgun to the agents and then walked with the two men to the barn, where he also handed over the fishing tackle box that contained the hunting knife. At the front door, she was told that her son had just confessed to the Clutter family murders. Until that moment, she told the court, she had no idea that he was implicated.

Next Agent Harold Docker took the stand. He confirmed having made several visits to the Hickock farm while investigating the case. When asked by Joseph Jenkins, the defense attorney, whether he had explained in any fashion what Mr. Hickock's rights were regarding a search warrant, he replied in a barely audible voice that he had not.

Replying to the same question, Agent Wayne Owens confirmed that the search was conducted without a warrant and the family's rights were never mentioned to them.

Neither details of the crime itself nor the guilt or innocence of Hickock and Smith were brought up at the hearing, which was focused entirely upon the two men's civil rights and the legal procedures employed to bring them to justice.

Subsequent witnesses included local newspaper and television personnel who had covered the investigation and the original trial and could testify regarding any heightened community prejudice against the fugitives that existed when they were returned to Garden City from Las Vegas. Their attorneys hoped to show that the court had erred when it failed to grant them a change of venue.

That day's session lasted well into the late evening hours. The final person to take the witness stand was defense attorney Harrison Smith, who had represented Richard Hickock in the original trial. He testified that his client told him he had given his confession freely and not under duress. "My chief interest," he told the court, "was in attempting to win the sentence of life in prison and not the death penalty for my client."

A recess was then called at 11 p.m.

Judge Templar had permitted a full exploration of all the facts surrounding Richard Hickock's and Perry Smith's arrests and trial. In summation, the defense attorneys hammered the points that the defendants' constitutional rights had been violated and that there were trial errors and the convicted men's punishment should be reduced to life in prison.

The prosecution's final argument, presented by Assistant Attorney General Richard Foth, was based upon the facts that both Hickock and Smith had admitted to the brutal murders and neither man had claimed they were intimidated or beaten or that promises had been made to them to obtain the confessions. He also believed that the court-appointed attorneys made the right decision in not seeking separate trials for the two defendants, saying, "Each confessed to killing two members of the Clutter family. How were the lawyers to know that one of them might not try to make a deal and sing like a bird and lay the blame on the other in hopes of getting life in prison?"

The ruling by Judge Templar came on October 23, 1963, in a 26-page opinion that stated, "I find no grounds for the Federal Courts to upset the death penalties of Richard Hickock or Perry Smith in the Clutter murder case were shown, and the murder verdicts should stand. I concluded that the petitioners failed to establish that their rights had been violated and that there was no miscarriage of justice."

Having found that none of the contentions had merit under a writ of *habeas corpus*, he vacated the stay of execution he had granted earlier. The death warrants issued by the Kansas Supreme Court could thus be restored. Judge Templar also ruled that the form of execution "death by hanging" did not amount to cruel and unusual punishment.

CHAPTER 17

The people of Kansas were on edge, and each time a new appeal or a new hearing was requested, Hickock's and Smith's date with the hangman was pushed back further and further. Many had begun to wonder whether the sentence given to them by the General District Court jury in Garden City back in 1960 would ever be carried out.

Now, a motion for a re-hearing was filed in United States District Court in Kansas City on behalf of Perry Smith. Richard Hickock's attorney was expected to initiate a similar action soon. This was a step that had to be taken before the men could have their cases heard by the 10th United States Court Of Appeals in Denver.

A Garden City Telegram editorial entitled "We Get The Message", published on December 27, 1963, reflects the mood at the time. In response to receiving an unsigned letter of criticism, the Editor wrote:

"It was an attack upon this county as 'some of the most spineless people in the world'. Our 'crime' is sitting back and not doing anything about two men in death row in the State Penitentiary – Richard Hickock and Perry Smith. 'You westerners along with your attorney general must be some of the most spineless people in the world,' the writer charged. If he is wondering why we didn't string them up on the courthouse lawn when they were returned here for trial, the question doesn't deserve an answer. If we are getting blamed for the legal actions taken on behalf of the convicted killers and the slow response of our courts, then the entire nation stands in the spotlight of the writer's accusation."

"While we are not satisfied by the inexcusable slow pace of the courts in the Hickock-Smith case, we don't think the two killers have escaped penalty for their crime, at least not yet. Life on death row is a living hell, we are told. Death is final but living in its shadows can be man's greatest torture. When the two do make the long trip to the gallows – and they will before long – it will be after every legal avenue of legal escape has been tried. They will have been afforded the due process of law guaranteed every citizen by our constitution."

"The eastern Kansas letter-writer may be surprised to hear we are civilized out this way to the point we have put away our six shooters and our ropes. But most of us are descent law-abiding citizens who believe in the rights of every man. And most have enough spine to sign their letters."

As Christmas approached, the cold Kansas nights brought snow, sleet and rain to Lansing. Life behind the maximum-security state penitentiary walls was the the same day and night, for months and years on end. But Christmas Day brought a small moment of hope to the 1,800 convicted prisoners, who could experience at least a small degree of kindness and joy.

The four death row inmates would be required to remain in their isolation cells all day. They were permitted to receive only three gifts each. Those could come only from family members and friends approved by the prison administration and were limited to candy, nuts, cigarettes, cigars and two books. Subject matter involving crime or sex was prohibited.

Richard Hickock, Perry Smith, James Douglas Latham and George Ronald York had all been convicted of multiple murders and were awaiting their trip to the gallows. Of the group, only Smith had no one to give him gifts and could only hope to get something special from the commissary.

The Christmas meal would consist of roast young tom turkey, snowflake potatoes, giblet gravy, celery dressing, buttered peas, cranberry sauce, half of a cling peach, fruit cake, hot rolls and butter and coffee. And that, for the condemned, was Christmas in 1963.

On January 10, attorneys for Hickock and Smith appeared before the 10th Circuit Court of Appeals to entered their pleas for retrial. Representing the State of Kansas at the hearing was Assistant Attorney General Arthur Palmer. Losing here would mean that the two killers would have only two options remaining on their long quest to try to save their lives: the United States Supreme Court or a grant of clemency from Kansas Governor John Anderson.

As the long string of appeals and hearings played out, the stress of isolation had begun to show on the two caged men. In a special report submitted to the warden concerning the mental state of Perry Smith, prison Chaplain James E. Post stated that after many counseling sessions he had found that the enormity of Smith's crime was weighing heavily on him. He was a terribly confused person and the victim of an unfortunate childhood filled with adversity and trauma.

A Kansas State Penitentiary Classification Study would show that the early years of the prisoner's life were far from normal. He was born in Huntington Valley, Nevada, on October 27, 1928, to John Tex "Buckaroo" Smith, of Dutch descent, and Florence "Flo" Julia Buckskin Smith, a full-blooded Shoshone.

John Tex Smith Florence Julia Buckskin Smith

The Shoshones of Northern Nevada were known as the "Snake Indians". The parents were performers and traveled the western states rodeo circuit as the "Flo & Tex Show", a bareback riding and roping team. That lifestyle meant constantly moving from one local venue to another with no real home except - at times - a homemade, fixer-upper trailer. They lived on welfare assistance for much of that time.

There were four children in the Smith family: Jimmy, Fern, Barbara, and Perry. Perry was the youngest. As the rodeo shows came to an end, Tex and Flo and their family moved to Juneau, Alaska, in 1929.

Perry's father distilled illegal bootleg whiskey to earn money until 1935, when he started becoming violent toward Flo and the four children. She had him arrested and jailed for domestic abuse. Once he was safely behind bars, she left, taking the truck and the family to San Francisco.

Soon, Flo's life also began to spiral out of control as she became more and more dependent upon alcohol and heaped abuse upon Perry and his siblings. Complications resulting from her excessive drinking caused her death when he was just 13, and the four children were then placed in a Catholic orphanage.

There, Perry claimed, he was abused both physically and mentally because of his chronic bedwetting, a condition that he said continued into adulthood and was attributed to malnutrition. During this period, being struck in the groin with a flashlight left him with a severe penis injury. As a teen, he also spent time in a Salvation Army orphanage, where the abuse continued.

One nurse in particular, he said, told him he was "just like a nigger and there was no difference between niggers and Indians." "Oh, Jesus, was she an evil bastard!" he recalled. "She would hold my head under water until I turned blue." These early years would set into motion a cycle of rejections, failures and criminal activities that kept Perry Smith in and out of jails and prisons for the remainder of his life.

Perry Smith

In an entry dated March 6, 1957, Captain S.H. Crouse recorded in the Kansas State Penitentiary files that in Perry Smith's first year of incarceration for burglary he had pled guilty to possessing a long list of contraband discovered in his prison cell # 228. In a routine check, prison guard Edward Goldin reported he found a homemade box with a hidden drawer, sandpaper, a twelve-inch ruler, a pair of pliers, a piece of a bandsaw blade, a piece of a file, a jar of glue, two pieces of a rubber innertube, a gambling roulette wheel, and a stinger.

In prison terms a "stinger" is a homemade device to heat water. Since hot water can be used as a weapon, they are not allowed in a prison setting. Most prison stingers are made from two pieces of wire from radio headsets or TV plugs and aluminum foil.

In his explanation, Smith stated that he was of a creative nature and liked to build things. The roulette wheel, he said, was for his own amusement in order to figure percentages. He had managed to obtain the other items through various departments within the institution.

In the prison report, Captain Crouse noted that Perry Smith appeared to be a very unstable individual who followed his own impulsive nature without weighing the consequences of his actions.

As a rehabilitative measure, the prison court recommended that he be held in isolation and then upon release be placed on thirty days of restriction. But the entire sentence could be avoided and set aside if Smith would show good behavior for a period of ninety days. The report also mentions that the young inmate was given extensive counseling regarding his actions. He was to have another run-in with the court in December of the following year. Found guilty of stealing ten cookies from the supper line, he was sentenced to 15 days of full restriction.

Perry Smith's long criminal history - burglary, grand larceny, jail break, and finally four counts of first-degree murder - earned him time in jails and prisons for a good portion of his adult life. In his parole hearing in 1959, he pleaded with the board for another chance at freedom, saying, "I intend to find and keep a good job; take certain steps to avoid situations that led to my imprisonment. Help my Father in his old age; and work for those things every man wants like a family and respect from decent people".

Asked on one form to describe his intentions if released, he wrote, "In the event I am paroled I plan to keep a steady job and readjust myself and become a useful member of society. At this time, I have no family responsibilities except to my Father who I am totally devoted. Plans for marriage and a happy family".

Smith's mental state and condition had been in question since the earliest days of his incarceration. In October of 1960, Doctor

Robert H. Moore, Medical Director of the Kansas State Penitentiary, had evaluated him and recommended that the death row inmate be transferred to the criminally insane ward at Larned State Hospital in Pawnee County for psychiatric evaluation and treatment.

Considering the safety concerns involved in his transfer and housing, however, the Classification Committee realized that Smith could pose a direct threat to innocent people involved in such a move. Instead, they recommended that the Director of Penal Institutions make necessary arrangements through the director of Institutional Management to have a competent group of psychiatrists and other medical experts visit Perry Smith and make a determination regarding his response to psychiatric treatment.

CHAPTER 18

On January 12, 1964, attorneys Joseph P. Jenkins and Robert Bingham stood before a three-judge panel of the U. S. 10th Circuit Court of Appeals in Denver, pleading with the jurists to consider a new trial for Hickock and Smith. Both held strong opinions that the defendants had been the victims of a nightmarishly unfair process. In their many attempts to get justice for them through through federal court system, they had given the two men at least a glimmer of hope that their lives could be spared.

The crux of the attorneys' argument was that the rights of neither of their clients had been protected. As a master orator of legal defense argument, Jenkins reminded the Court that Richard Hickock had not been appointed an attorney until after he had confessed to the crimes he had been accused of, adding that Hickock had waived his right to a preliminary hearing with no counsel.

He also told the panel that his client had not been competently represented at his trial and was convicted with the help of evidence seized without a search warrant. Furthermore, he argued, the two men were not granted a change of trial location even though Garden

City had been saturated with publicity prejudiced against the accused.

It took only two days for the panel to announce their ruling. Hickock and Smith learned that they had been granted additional hearings and the court had ordered a certificate of probable cause.

When newspapers broke the story, local residents who thought the end was finally in sight were once again left troubled and weary. An editorial titled "Something Is Wrong" in the Garden City Telegram stated, "Numerous court actions have put off their executions.' This was the concluding statement in a story reported concerning the latest delay in the hanging of James Latham and George York, two young killers who were convicted and sentenced to die back in 1961. It is the same statement which could be used in a story of two other killers, Richard Hickock and Perry Smith."

"It is not with revenge that we patiently await the end of these cases. The hanging of these four men will not bring the several victims back to life. But the animal existence of the four on death row in Lansing is not serving any purpose other than to keep them out of society where they didn't fit. They are not being rehabilitated, if that is even possible in these cases. Nor are they doing anything productive. What has delayed their executions is not a question of their guilt, which has been established without doubt and to all which they have admitted. The issues with fair trials and adequate counsel have kept these men alive. Yet there is little doubt that they all had fair trials."

"With confessions of guilt and conclusive evidence, there are few if any attorneys in the country who could have defended them successfully. We cannot blame the defendants from trying to evade the gallows, but there is something basically wrong with a judiciary system which allows these incredible delays that leaves both them and the public in doubt for several years."

Mack Nations

In 1961, Starling Mack Nations was a reporter working for the Wichita Eagle and Beacon. Born in 1919, he had learned all phases of the newspaper business from his father, Hobart McKinley Nations, City Editor of the Marshall Democrat-News in Missouri and then owner and publisher of the Greensburg News.

Tuberculosis took the life of the elder Nations in 1933, and Mack dropped out of school to help run the business. After returning to finish his education at Kansas Wesleyan Junior College in Salina and then Pratt Junior College, he started his own newspaper in Chase,

Kansas. The first edition of The Chase Index was published on March 21, 1946.

By 1950, Nations had sold his interest in that paper and others and was doing courthouse reporting for the Wichita Eagle and Beacon. It was through that job that his story and those of Hickock and Smith became intertwined.

Assigned to write a feature article on the State Penitentiary's death row inmates, he requested and was granted permission by the facility administration to conduct interviews with them on prison grounds. During his conversation with Richard Hickock, the convicted killer surprised him by saying he'd be willing to collaborate on a book telling his life story and revealing for the first time the details of the brutal crimes he and Smith had committed.

Recognizing the potential of such an explosive tell-all memoir, Nations agreed to participate. After many lengthy visits and over two hundred letters written by Hickock, the two agreed to have Garden City attorney Dale H. Corley draw up a legal contract. The terms specified that they would split any and all proceeds 50/50.

Hickock's motivation was to raise funds he needed to finance the services of a competent attorney that could guide his case through the appeals process and a possible new trial to reverse his sentence and to help support his Mother. He would spend the next six months writing the manuscript in longhand. The first draft was over a hundred thousand pages long, with a working title of "High Road To Hell".

Just a few months after signing the contract, however, Richard Hickock was made aware of a new directive issued by Col. Guy C. Rexroad, Director of Kansas Penal Institutions. In it, he decreed that no inmate in the system would be allowed to correspond in any way with members of the news media.

By now a prolific letter-writer, Hickock sent a lengthy response pleading that he be allowed to continue his interaction with Nations for the benefit of both his legal defense and his ailing parent. And his was not the only challenge to Rexroad's new policy.

On October 19, 1961, the Director received a letter from a prestigious Kansas law firm, announcing that they would be representing the interests of Truman Capote, a highly-respected writer from New York City. It went on to explain that Capote had come to the state in November of 1959 to investigate the possibility of creating a series of articles on the murders for New Yorker magazine. He had done extensive research, using records at Kansas State University and other sources to develop background information on the victims, attended the initial trial, and stayed in touch with the case throughout the lengthy appeals process.

Capote's story had already been accepted by the magazine and was also set to be published in book form by Random House. The attorneys argued that "Mr. Capote feels to complete his work it is essential and imperative that he be allowed to interview both Richard Hickock and Perry Smith at the State Penitentiary at Lansing. Our law firm sent a letter to Warden Tracy Hand of The Kansas State Penitentiary asking that a date could be agreed that Mr. Capote could interview both inmates. Our office received a reply on October 16, 1961, from Warden Hand explaining that the rules and regulations of the Penitentiary could not permit an interview and any other correspondence concerning this matter should be sent directly to Director Col. Rexroad's office in Topeka."

"We are not unmindful of the necessities of rules and regulations of this type in running an institution such as the one at Lansing. And if this were a new venture by an inexperienced writer, we would not make this request. However, since Mr. Capote did commence his study and research of this case some time ago now and we feel he is attempting to do everything possible to develop a comprehensive presentation of this incident, we feel we have just grounds to ask that your office to waive the rules and regulations in this particular case."

"It is common knowledge that other writers have been allowed in the past to interview these two inmates, so we believe that it is in their best interest and the public's general interest that Mr. Capote be allowed to interview these two men. It is widely known that Mr. Capote is a writer of very high stature. In other words, we know Mr. Capote's story will not be of the pulp magazine variety but on the other hand will be written on a much higher plane than this. We would like for you to examine this matter and give us a favorable decision. We would like for Mr. Capote to be able to interview both Hickock and Smith in January of 1962."

CHAPTER 19

For Hickock's plea, the determination would come from Kansas State Attorney General William M. Ferguson. In a letter to Rexroads dated December 1, 1961, he ruled in favor of the prisoner. According to Kansas Statute 70 Kan. 429 Grey vs Stewart, he stated, an inmate serving a life sentence was considered civilly dead. But strict interpretation of that law meant that it could not be applied to one awaiting execution. This loophole allowed Richard Hickock to resume his personal business dealings with Mack Nations.

The Attorney General also mentioned that the Hickock story had been published in the December issue of Male Magazine and the article included a statement that the Kansas inmate was being treated very unfairly by the prison administration. He made it perfectly clear that this type of negative publicity was not what the Attorney General's Office wanted or would tolerate. It was also mentioned that Hickock should be allowed to correspond with others concerning his story and denying him this privilege would appear to support of his claim of unfair treatment.

Finally, Rexroad was instructed to make Richard Hickock aware that if he now speaks with or corresponds with Mr. Capote or any other writer he may be in breach of contract with Mr. Nations and lose any financial gain he would have been entitled to.

On the morning of October 6, 1961, the Garden City Telegram revealed that Nations was preparing a book that had been accepted by Random House and a national magazine would be publishing a condensed version. Based upon hundreds of hours of interviews, it was to be Richard Hickock's move-by-move, emotion-by-emotion account of the period from five to six days before the crime until his days in the penitentiary.

Many in the Garden City area and other parts of Kansas were deeply concerned by the possibility that the killer would be receiving monetary gain from the horrific brutal crime for which he had been convicted.

Who would get the legal rights to put the story into print? The local newspaper reporter or the up-and-coming New York writer? In the end, of course, Truman Capote's In Cold Blood was a worldwide success – first as a book and then as a film. Readers would finally have their long-awaited close-up look at the two men who confessed to the killings. But before that, an interesting battle played out for months behind the scenes. The details were largely ignored and kept from the public.

When the content of the Nations manuscript became known, many saw it as a work of complete fiction and a shameless attempt to make money. Letters in the Kansas State Penitentiary archives describe "High Road To Hell" as telling a tale that wasn't at all supported by the facts of the case – one that characterized the Clutter killings as a murder-for-hire plot.

A man named "Roberts" had supposedly contracted with Richard Hickock and Perry Smith to kill Mr. Clutter for a fee of five thousand dollars. The narrative described the murders in bloody and horrific detail. After Perry Smith shot young Kenyan Clutter directly in the face, Hickock supposedly said, "I'd like to see the embalmer fill that hole".

The Hickock manuscript was never published. The aforementioned Male Magazine article was an excerpt sold to that publication by Nations, and it mentioned nothing of the supposed plot. Richard Hickock and Perry Smith were named in the story as two unrepentant lowlife thug murderers who deserved to be hung for the brutal acts they had committed on an innocent family of four. Most considered Hickock's work to be largely fiction, concocted by a pathological liar. Nations conveyed it personally to Random House Publishing in New York City but soon thereafter received a letter of rejection based upon the fact that they had already signed a contract with Truman Capote.

It was a bitter loss for the reporter, who had invested tremendous time and effort in the project. He expected Hickock's book to be one of his writing career's most significant achievements. Records show that he felt cheated and believed that politics had played a major role in Colonel Rexroad's decision to waive his new rule and allow Capote to interview the two killers in Lansing. And there may have been some basis in fact for his thinking. Correspondence the authors found in the prison archives offers a clue.

Two of the principals of the law firm intervening on Capote's behalf were State Representatives Clifford Ragdale Hope and Dale Saffels, who would later be appointed a Federal court judge. In the initial letter sent to Saffels by Rexroad, their request had been denied. Later, however, that decision was suddenly reversed. One can only speculate whether this wording appended to the attorneys' request was influential: "Colonel Rexroad, I am, of course, very much interested in the situation at Hutchinson Reformatory and sincerely hope at the completion of the investigation there that it will be determined that many of the accusations and much of the publicity which has occurred are not based on fact. Yours truly, Dale Saffels".

Once the news reached Mack Nations that Truman Capote would be allowed to interview both Hickock and Smith, he wrote on Wichita Eagle and Beacon letterhead to penitentiary Warden Tracy Hand. Found in the prison archives, his letter reads:

"Dear Sir: I have been informed by Col. Guy Rexroad that he has granted permission to Truman Capote, a writer from New York, to interview Richard Hickock. Inasmuch as the present prison rules prohibit all other writers including myself from seeing or corresponding with Hickock, I would appreciate very much you conveying the following information to Richard Eugene Hickock: 'Under terms of the contract between Richard Eugene Hickock and Mack Nations to edit and make ready for publication the story of Richard Eugene Hickock's life, said Richard Eugene Hickock granted to Mack Nation exclusive rights to any and all of the story forever.'"

"The Terms of which that contract was drawn at the request of Richard Eugene Hickock have been and are still being carried out by

Mack Nations in every detail. In the event that Richard Eugene Hickock violates, verbally or otherwise with and by giving interviews concerning his life story to Truman Capote or any other person, Richard Eugene Hickock automatically forfeits his one half the contract calling for him to receive of any and all moneys received from the sale of the story by Mack Nations."

"I would also like Mr. Hickock informed that any or all moneys received from Mr. Capote, or any other writer for information of his life which violates this contract will be impounded insofar as legally possible pending a damage suit outcome which will be files against him by Mack Nations. If you will be so kind as to give Mr. Hickock this information and acknowledge such to me I will be grateful. Yours truly, Mack Nations".

This letter from Mack Nations would prove to be extremely helpful and would open the door for him to resume communication with Richard Hickock - but only under the strictest prison guidelines. Correspondence would be limited to that of a business nature only. Nothing would be allowed that would add to what material Nations already had concerning Richard Hickock's life story.

Just months after Nations had made his attempts to have the Hickock manuscript published, he was arrested and charged with federal tax evasion. A grand jury in Topeka found that he had falsified his 1962 tax return and evaded paying taxes on $1200. After a lengthy trial, Nations was acquitted of the charges. But he was left financially troubled and his reputation was tainted.

It was said that during this difficult period of Mack Nation's life, Truman Capote had learned of the charges and said to friends, "Have you heard about that bastard Mack Nations? The one who gave me so much trouble? He's been arrested for tax evasion".

Where is Hickock's "High Road To Hell" manuscript? No one seems to know. It was in Mack Nations' possession for many years, and then he gave it to his mother for safekeeping. When he had moved and was co-owner, editor and publisher of the Huerfona World Newspaper in Walensburg, Colorado, he took ownership once again.

Late on December 24 of 1968, Nations left his desk and headed home for the Christmas holiday. Six miles west of Aguilar, Colorado, in Las Animas County, he was killed in a single-vehicle accident. State Police reported that his car went out of control, hit a concrete abutment and came to rest in a drainage ditch. His funeral was held at Fleeners Chapel, and he was buried in Greensburg, Kansas.

Years later, his son Michael said, "We never saw my father's original manuscript again or ever knew what happened to it".

CHAPTER 20

Meanwhile, on the editorial pages of Kansas newspapers, the drumbeat of discontent continued:

"The Long Wait Begins"

The Garden City Telegram, October 9, 1961

"A Kansas District Court sentences two more young men to the gallows. Again, those who oppose capital punishment can find fodder for their crusade with the prospect of two young men falling through a trap door at the end of a rope. But much of the sting of these death sentences is removed by the remoteness of the climb of the gallows steps.

It soon will be two years since Richard Hickock and Perry Smith murdered the four members of the Clutter Family in cold blood in Holcomb. They were sentenced to hang by a Finney County District Court jury in April of 1960."

"Since then, the two condemned men who admitted the crime and were found guilty beyond a shadow of a doubt, have been living on death row at Lansing while going through the slow process of higher appeals. Hickock has sold his story on how he committed the crime, published in a current magazine, in an effort to raise money to continue his defense."

"Opponents of capital punishment claim it has not been a deterrent to crime. But the oft-used avenue to escape through insanity and the long delays that can stretch over several years offer hope to all killers of beating the death rap. In an effort to protect the innocent, our laws can sometimes provide breaks for the guilty."

On July 8, 1961, the Kansas Supreme Court ruled that both Hickock and Smith had received fair trials. The unanimous opinion was written by Chief Justice Jay Parker. In it, he explained that the court, after reading the entire trial transcript as well as the abstracts of the representing parties, had failed to find any plain error - whether specified or not - that would justify or require the reversal of their convictions.

In their motions for a new trial, both Hickock and Smith through their representing attorneys had contended that they had not received a fair trial because the trial court had failed to appoint at least one psychiatrist to a commission of three physicians who examined them. The three commissioned doctors had found, after a thorough examination, that Richard Hickock and Perry Smith were both sane and did know right from wrong at the time of the murders and could stand trial.

Chief Justice Parker noted that at trial a psychiatrist testifying on behalf of the defendants stated his belief that Richard Hickock knew right from wrong but offered no opinion on whether the same was true of Perry Smith.

The defense had also brought the claim that the defendants did not receive a fair and impartial trial due to the overwhelming media coverage by local and state and national news outlets. The high court, after a close examination of the trial transcripts, could find no evidence whatsoever that either defendant had ever claimed or indicated that he was being deprived of a fair and impartial trial by the news media.

Headlines across the state of Kansas proclaimed "Killers Fail In Move To Escape Death". Indeed, the Kansas high court decision virtually precluded any further moves by the two men in state courts. Now, defense attorney Russell Shultz stated his intention to take the case to the United States Supreme Court and, if it failed there, to the U. S. Court of Appeals.

But Kansas Supreme Court documents reveal that both Hickock and Smith had been very unhappy with Shultz and wanted him removed from their case. In his place, they wished to have a fellow penitentiary inmate represent them. The Supreme Court denied the request, saying only members of the Kansas Bar were allowed to argue on behalf of clients before that body.

The two convicted murderers' only hope now lay in the Federal court system. And Richard Hickock had begun to realize that time was running out and he would need the very best legal representation in order to save his life.

In September of 1962, Perry Smith unexpectedly filed for an appeal through newly- appointed United States Supreme Court Justice Byron R. White. Justice White denied his petition in the first week of October, paving the way for Smith to be hanged on October

25 in accordance with the terms of his death sentence. The condemned killer was heard to say, "I will go it alone", stating that he would seek no further appeals and would not try to delay his date with the executioner. But in another attempt to delay justice just hours before he was to be hanged, he filed an appeal with United States District Judge Arthur J. Stanely, Jr., and was granted a stay of execution.

Judge Stanely also appointed Attorney Joseph P. Jenkins of Kansas City to represent Richard Hickock. Now, the legal process would once again grind to halt until Jenkins could present his case before the United States Supreme Court in Washington.

The death penalty remained a topic of controversy in the fall of 1962. Many of the leading statewide newspapers regularly ran editorials on the subject. One, entitled "Realistic Answer", argued passionately against capital punishment after the execution of Lloyd Lee Andrews but then undercut its own position by stating that an exception should be made for Hickock and Smith. The writer went on to explain:

"There is no doubt others in this area who have a Christian conviction against taking another man's life in payment for his crime against society, but because of the closeness and the brutality of the Clutter case would ask that an exception be made for Hickock and Smith."

"It often is easier to rationalize than fight with your conscience. Another killer was due to hang on Kansas gallows a few years ago but was given a last-minute reprieve by then Kansas Governor George Docking. His death sentence was commuted to life imprisonment, and since then he has killed again inside the prison walls. It's obvious we have not advanced to the point where we can mend all criminal minds and make peaceful citizens out of cold-blooded killers. Keeping them within the maximum confines of our prisons is not helping them or benefiting society—with the exception of protection."

"Forgiveness does not mean we must not always punish. Putting the offenders behind prison walls is society's way of shutting the door on a problem it does not have the answer to or does not worry about. But there comes a time when we must face reality. As punishment for some crimes, capital punishment is the only realistic answer."

On June 26, 1963, the Kansas Supreme Court had set the newest execution date for the two to be August 8. Their appeals to the United States Supreme Court had been denied earlier that year. Attorney Joseph P. Jenkins set in motion another legal maneuver by appealing to the United States District Court that neither defendant had been appointed legal counsel until twelve days after their arrest in Las Vegas.

He claimed that their confessions were obtained in violation of their civil rights, they did not have proper legal counsel at their trials, the evidence upon which their convictions were based was obtained illegally, and both men should have been granted a change of venue. Judge George Templar would preside over the hearing.

On August 2, Judge Templar granted a stay of execution for both Richard Hickock and Perry Smith. Harrison Smith, Richard Hickock's legal counsel in the original murder trial, testified that Hickock told him that he gave his confession freely and voluntarily and that no duress had been used. He further stated that his chief goal had been to win life in prison in lieu of the death penalty for his client.

Also appearing was Roy Church, Agent for the Kansas Bureau of Investigation, who described in detail the circumstances surrounding Richard Hickock's confession and his return trip to Garden City to stand trial. Judge Roland Tate, the presiding judge at the first trial, was also called to the stand as a witness for the State of Kansas.

After the two-day hearing, Judge Templar denied the convicted murderers' appeal, telling the court he could find no grounds on which to grant the request. But mere days after the decision was announced, newspapers across Kansas informed their readers that the attorneys for the two killers would be filing yet another application for a re-hearing on the matter in Topeka. That would be a prerequisite for an appeal to the United States Court of Appeals in Denver Colorado.

To many in the Garden City area, this came as no surprise. Many had come to accept the many delays with a shrug of resignation – unable to comprehend the slow movement of justice but realizing there was nothing they could do about it. Some expressed deep concerns that Hickock and Smith would live to a ripe old age at taxpayers' expense.

The years spent in cold, cramped isolation cells dragged on slowly, taking their toll on the penitentiary's death row inmates. Non-stop screaming and profanity assaulted their ears, driving many to the point of considering suicide. For Richard Hickock, letter writing was the only escape. He spent long hours sitting on his steel bunk with his pencil and paper. In many of the letters written during this period that have been preserved for historical review, we learn that the convicted murderer constantly longed for the use of a radio.

In his mind, if the men on death row could only have that one privilege, it would help restore some sanity to the nightmare situation they found themselves in. Hickock in particular dreamed of enjoying Saturday afternoon broadcasts of baseball games. He also mentioned listening to Kansas University football games and soothing, easy listening music on Sunday evenings to take his mind off the harsh reality of how his life was likely to end.

His mother lent her support to the cause. In a heartfelt letter to Robert J. Kaiser, Director of Kansas Penile Institutions, dated September 17, 1963, she wrote:

"Dear Sir. Would it be possible for the men on death row at Lansing Kansas to have a radio? I have a son there sorry to say. He is very depressed and despondent. I found this out when I was up there. He had written me a two-page letter concerning his health and welfare. I did not get it. I can understand they are not in a place like that for pleasure. But after all they are human beings. And will have to pay for the crime they did. And I do think maybe just a little kindness would help them. I would be willing to pay for the radio. Thank you for reading my letter I hope you will give it some consideration. Yours Truly Eunice Hickock".

JENKINS MUS
RADIOS
11.00
11.95

CHAPTER 21

The citizens of Kansas continued to voice their displeasure at how slowly the process to execute convicted murderers in their state seemed to move:

"The Cruelty of Delay", by Whitley Austin

The Salina Journal
October 14, 1963

"We have voiced deep concern about the too-long course of justice such as in the Perry Smith and Richard Hickock case. Most of this area share this concern, as do some other newspaper editors. Four years ago next month, four members of a prominent farm family were brutally shot to death in their home near Holcomb in Southwestern Kansas. For these murders Richard Hickock and Perry Smith were arrested tried and convicted and sentenced to death."

"Except for those who prohibit capital murder under any circumstances, it was the consensus that society could protect itself from such men only by eliminating them. Their backgrounds, their prison records, the cold-blooded unprovoked murder itself, all indicated them to be an intolerable menace.

Those that oppose the death penalty, however, argue that society is the real criminal in the case, that we have collectively failed in education and reform and that the slayings should be upon all our consciences. In part this is true, although it does not mitigate the crime or make execution of the murders less justified."

"Now we collectively have another matter on our consciences. After a series of appeals and technical arguments the case of Smith and Hickock is still before the courts. Their guilt is not in question, but the technicality of their convictions seems to be."

"Four years is too long. Unreasonable too long, cruelly too long for the course of law to take. Certainly, the pair deserved every chance of appeal, every protection of the law; no one asks cottonwood justice. But to spin out the procedure until the case threatens to outlive evidence and witnesses, to delay the operation of the law is an outrage on justice."

"It is a manner of thwarting the law, reducing its effectiveness, of bringing discredit upon it. The various judges, lawyers and clerks and their suicidal habits of procrastination may be directly to blame. However, it should also be on our consciences that we permit the law to be mocked in this sad fashion."

The issue of allowing death row inmates use of a transistor radio took on new importance with a very straightforward and somewhat threatening letter from Richard Hickock's court-appointed attorney Joseph P. Jenkins to the Director of Prisons, dated June 19, 1964.

Referencing the intolerable conditions that the death row inmates at the Kansas State Penitentiary at Lansing must endure, Jenkins wrote:

"As you know a man waiting to be hanged, but who has appeals pending, while he should not be given the comforts of home, he should be treated tolerable. Cruel and unusual punishment went out in the dark ages. It is my understanding that one of the things that concerns prison officials is discipline. But I fail to comprehend how such discipline can be attained under the conditions now existing in death row at Lansing. I know that death row is not a separate building but that other inmates are kept at the same location for other disciplinary reasons. But in any event, I believe penologists through out the country would condemn this type of imprisonment you have imposed on Richard Hickock and the four other men on death row at Lansing."

"It seems most fundamental that a caged man would soon become a mental problem if not given things to keep him busy. These men are not allowed any exercise outside of their death row cells. They are allowed only one paperback book per week. They have been repeatedly denied the use of a transistor radio. How can it be explained to anyone why your officials at the Kansas penitentiary took all of Mr. Hickock's court documents that he personally purchased from the West Publishing Company and other legal documents that were taken from his cell and destroyed?"

"I personally know that Mr. Hickock dabbles in painting. He had requested that I give him photographs of members of my family so he could paint portraits of them. He said this could be some compensation for the services I had rendered him and that being able to paint would help him keep his mind busy in his isolation cell."

"I believe an explanation is forthcoming to why his art supplies were taken from him and some even destroyed. What justification can there be for denying a condemned man the right to paint pictures? I have mentioned the matter of the transistor radios to Warden Crouse and asked him to take the matter up with you and your office. And nothing has been done."

"Warden Crouse informed me that the final decision concerning the transistor radios would have to come from you and your office. I believe that the courts assess punishments and this punishment is carried out only by prison officials. The social science of penology has made great strides in the past twenty years, but frankly I believe the state of Kansas has overlooked what other states of done. I respectfully request an answer to this letter and that some steps be made to make life more tolerable for Mr. Hickock and the other four men on Kansas's death row at Lansing."

"If nothing is done concerning these matters, I will have no alternative but to take this matter up with the Governor. If I get nowhere there, I believe this is a matter for the newspapers and perhaps for the courts. I am no crusader, but I do feel our prison system should measure up to other states. Respectfully, Joseph P. Jenkins."

The back-and-forth correspondence between Richard Hickock and Kansas State Penitentiary Warden Tracy Hand and Warden Sherman Crouse and Colonel Guy Rexroad concerning the radio request had dragged on since April of 1962. It would be James McAtee, the Director of Kansas State Penal Institutions, who would finally give permission for each death row inmate to have use of a transistor radio to be used only with earphones. It was one of the very few victories Richard Hickock achieved in his lengthy stay on death row, and it came just weeks before his execution.

The next hearing, before the United States 10th Circuit Court of Appeals in Denver, took place on January 10, 1964. A three-judge panel heard the pleas from attorneys for Richard Hickock and Perry Smith that their clients' constitutional rights had been violated and the two had been unfairly tried in Finney County District Court in Garden City. In a ruling announced on October 1st, both Hickock and Smith were granted the right to file petitions at the United States Supreme Court for writs of *certiorari*. If this petition were granted, the high court would call up for review the records of the lower courts.

Just over three months after the Supreme Court had provided a time frame for filing the petitions, on January 18, 1965, they announced their refusal to review the trials from lower courts. This was the second time the highest court in the United States had rejected an appeal from Richard Hickock and Perry Smith.

Acting quickly, Robert H. Bingham, legal counsel for Perry Smith, asked Justice Byron M. White to stay the executions pending court action on a plea that the tribunal reconsider its decision. His request was denied when the Supreme Court had convened for its next session on March 1. Now, the two condemned men had but one possible way left to try to save their lives.

In a news release, Kansas Governor William H. Avery reported that the attorney for Richard Hickock had made a request to defer his execution, scheduled for April 14. The Governor gave no indication as to what action he would take on the request. The reprieve was to allow time for a clemency hearing before the state Board of Pardons and Paroles. He also mentioned that he had not received any request from the counsel for Perry Smith but expected that he would. Governor Avery pointed out that a thirty-day notice is required for a clemency hearing in the state of Kansas and that there would not be sufficient time left before the execution date unless a reprieve were granted.

CHAPTER 22

On March 31st, the Garden City Telegram published requests for a clemency hearing from both Hickock and Smith. If Governor Avery granted the delay, a clemency hearing would be scheduled for April 29th. The newspaper's editorial page described the turn of events as follows:

"An Oversight"

Garden City Telegram

April 1, 1965

"Either an oversight or a deliberate planning may give convicted murderers Richard Hickock and Perry Smith an extension on life. The two are scheduled or were scheduled to die on the gallows at the Kansas State Penitentiary in Lansing on April 14. Their attorneys are seeking a clemency hearing before Governor William Avery. But a notice of application for such a hearing must be posted thirty days prior to the hearing date. This notice first appeared yesterday in this newspaper with a hearing date of April 29th. So Governor Avery must grant a reprieve for at least fifteen days if he agrees to the hearing."

"Many from here and other places in the state will oppose the application for executive clemency. There also will be those with strong convictions against capital punishment who will urge the Governor to grant clemency. We do not feel the Governor should do this unless some new evidence came to his attention which either cast a doubt on the guilt of the two men or gave some other legitimate reason the two should not hang. Governor Avery is in a spot he should not be placed. He has the power to determine if two men should live or die. The law should allow him to make this decision only on the basis of evidence rather than person conviction."

On Monday April 5, 1965, headlines across Kansas and the entire United States blared that the Governor had denied the reprieve. He had letters sent to attorneys Joseph Jenkins and Attorney Robert Bingham, explaining that he had "given careful and serious consideration to the requests submitted to me on behalf of Richard Hickock and Perry Smith, who are presently under the sentence of death after having been convicted of four counts of murder in the first degree by a jury in Finney County, Kansas. I have also given consideration to the oral presentation in the support of the application by Mr. Jenkins and Mr. Bingham on April 1, 1965. I have concluded a reprieve should not be granted on the application, and you are here by notified in writing of my decision denying the application."

On Tuesday morning, April 6th, both attorneys were back in Finney County District Court filing for an appeal under a new Code of Civil Procedure and asking that both men's death sentences be set aside. District Judge Alex Hotchkiss of Lyndon, Kansas, would oversee the proceedings. In the hearing, attorney Bingham expressed his belief that neither Hickock nor Smith had received a fair trial five years ago. He claimed that many of the allegations he would be presenting had never been explored in depth in any court.

The attorneys asked the court for a continuance to allow them more time to analyze that information. They also requested that both Hickock and Smith be returned to the same courtroom in which they had been convicted five years earlier and that all of the members of the trial jury be brought back as well.

Standing before Judge Hotchkiss, attorney Jenkins read a long list of reasons the two men had not received a fair trial: (1) misconduct by counselors Arthur Fleming and Harrison Smith; (2) misconduct by Duane West, the County Attorney and prosecutor; (3) prejudicial pre-trial publicity regarding the case and especially from the Garden City Telegram; (4) unnecessary delay in appointing council for the two men; (5) failure to obtain search warrants for the Hickock home and the car the two men drove to Las Vegas when they were arrested; (6) community prejudice; and (7) refusing to give each man a physiological examination. Attorney Jenkins contended that none of those things had been dealt with adequately.

Attorney Bingham, shaking his head, recounted that prosecuting attorney West had held between 24 and 26 news conferences before the trial had even begun and that the Garden City Telegram had published photos on the front page showing the shotgun allegedly used to murder the Clutter family, along with photos of the adhesive tape and the cords used to bind the victims - all before the trial had taken place.

Addressing the court in a firm voice, Jenkins said that the prosecuting attorney did not protest this deluge of prejudicial information and in fact had contributed to it. In closing, he contended that the newspaper's pre-trial story had made it impossible for the men to get a fair trial in Finney County.

On Friday morning, April 9th, Judge Hotchkiss announced his decision. He denied the motion that the two condemned men's sentences should be set aside. Once again, Hickock and Smith had lost their attempt to get a ruling that would have spared their lives and canceled their date with the Kansas hangman.

Explaining his judgment, Hotchkiss said that the motion showed no new or different grounds for relief not already presented and determined in the *habeas corpus* brought before the State Supreme Court or the US District Court and thereafter considered on appeals, and that all grounds urged have been completely considered and decided.

Moments after the ruling, attorneys Jenkins and Bingham stood and asked the court for the right to appeal it before the Kansas Supreme Court. Their request was granted.

Rushing from the courtroom, the attorneys stopped only long enough to tell the waiting news reporters, "It's not over. Before this day ends, we'll be knocking on the door at the Kansas Supreme Court." Legal papers in hand, they left the District Courthouse by car to start their 320-mile journey across the state to Topeka. Arriving with just minutes to spare, they were able to file their motion. A hearing was scheduled for Monday, April 12th.

Meanwhile, the scheduled execution date drew ever closer. Governor Avery had agreed to allow a clemency hearing before himself and the Kansas Board of Probation and Parole, to be held behind closed doors at the penitentiary subject to the tightest security measures. Board Chairman C. H. Looney would allow no one to attend except Board members and the two condemned men and their attorneys, with two exceptions: Richard Hickok's mother Eunice and his brother Walter could be present. This would be the convicted killers' one last attempt to convince the Governor and the Board of Probation and Parole to spare their lives.

Pleading on his own behalf, Richard Hickock spoke for an hour and thirty minutes. He repeatedly stated that he had not killed anyone in the early morning hours of November 15, 1959, and that there was never any premeditation. He insisted that it was a planned robbery and nothing more. He said that it was Perry Smith who had killed all four members of the Clutter family and he had no idea of what was happening once the killings had begun. Records would reveal that the Board members delved into every aspect of the case.

When called upon to speak, Eunice Hickock had little to say except that she could not explain her son's actions. She told the Governor that she believed the chances for his rehabilitation were good and that she felt he would make a good citizen. She described the automobile accident Richard had survived as a youngster and stated that she had felt after the accident that he had mental problems from the severe head injuries he had sustained from the crash. The weary mother of Richard Hickock sat with her shoulders slumped over her frail, thin body. Years of pain and agony and shame were etched in the lines of her face. Her voice was soft and almost inaudible.

Finishing her remarks to Governor Avery, she was heard to say, “May God be with you while you make your deliberations.” After the hearing was over, attorney Jenkins told waiting reporters that Mrs. Hickock had broken down only once during the closed-door proceedings, saying that she never begged or pleaded and calling her a very remarkable woman.

CHAPTER 23

At long last, it was over. On Tuesday, April 13th, headlines across Kansas announced that the Governor would not intervene in the execution of Richard Hickock and Perry Smith scheduled for April 14 at midnight. In a short statement, he said, "After weighing all matters and giving much thought and consideration and fully considering this application, I have come to the conclusion that the application for clemency for Richard Hickock and Perry Smith should be denied." He also confirmed that that the Board of Probation and Parole had recommended denial. The executions would now proceed as scheduled.

Both condemned men were notified by prison Deputy Warden Kenneth Harton of the Governor's actions. Reports from Lansing described Hickock and Smith as being in good spirits and talkative. The end of their long, exhausting wait was now in sight. For the most part, the prison staff never really expected this to be the way things would end. Many had assumed that both men's sentences would be reduced to life in prison.

Around mid-afternoon on April 13th, both Hickock and Smith were taken from their cells and escorted to the Captain's office, where they were placed in separate holding rooms. With only hours left to live, Richard Hickock was still in a joking mood. When one of the prison guards offered him a cigarette, he turned it down, saying, "Oh, no...they cause cancer." In another light moment, someone said, "Dick, this must be the longest night of your life." And Hickock replied, "No, I think it might be the shortest," and giggled.

Warden Sherman Crouse informed both Hickock and Smith that who would be executed first would be determined by alphabetical order or, if they choose, the flip of a coin. They opted for the coin flip. Corrections officer Greg Collins recalled years later that Richard Hickock had won the flip. With a broad grin, he looked up and commented, "Well I'll be damned. The first thing I ever won in my life".

Meanwhile, in the other room, Perry Smith sat with prison Chaplain James Post. In a much more solemn frame of mind, he talked quietly about life and death and how he felt he had something to contribute to life, but it was "all over now." He was consoled by by the chaplain.

Only hours before the executions were to be carried out, Deputy Warden Kenneth Harton had come to the death row cells and had both men brought to a pale grey room that contained one table with four metal chairs. Once they were seated, he told them he was there to ask what they wanted to request for their final meals.

After a long pause, Richard Hickock looked at Perry Smith and said, "Let's have some of those big, broiled shrimps, and make them spicy. And what about a big pile of French fries?" Smith chimed in, "Yeah, how about some garlic bread and some hot rolls and Coca

Colas and strawberry sodas?" And they agreed on a dessert of vanilla ice cream and strawberries with whipped cream.

The clock was counting down the minutes. At 10:30 p.m., the two men were taken to separate rooms and served their meals in the company of prison chaplains.

Some of the prison guards who were present described what transpired in those last remaining hours. Both men returned to their death row cells and began gathering all the personal items they had accumulated over the last five and half years. One of the guards said that Hickock wanted to give him all of his sports books, and another reported that Perry Smith had given him a small purse, which he kept for many years.

Midnight was approaching. In the guard room, those chosen to be apart of the execution squad now realized that the process was indeed going to move forward. Both Hickock and Smith were placed in a large, heavy harnesses made of thick leather with steel double-locking wrist shackles to restrain their hands and arms within. When the straps were tightened, Richard Hickock fell silent and his face turned pale white. And then he unexpectedly requested that his corneas be donated to the Kansas University Medical Center.

Perry Smith was noticeably nervous. When he had been secured in his harness, he asked Warden Sherman Crouse if he could he use the bathroom one last time. His request was quickly denied, but the warden was overruled by the director of Kansas Penal Institutions Chuck McAtee.

At 11:45 p.m., a grey Kansas State Penitentiary car pulled up outside the prison entrance, arriving in silence and what some witnesses described as slow motion. A bright light shone above the door, illuminating the tiny, misty raindrops falling from the night sky.

Suddenly two guards appeared, wearing brimmed hats and holding the arms of Richard Hickock. A fog had set in. Approaching the vehicle, the prisoner stopped to take one last look up into the darkness, letting the light rain fall on his face. Then, placing him in the center of the back seat, the guards climbed in on both sides.

It would be just a short drive to the dimly-lit warehouse connected to the penitentiary's outer wall. The door was open, and a group waited silently inside. All of them wore overcoats and hats. Outside, there were several Kansas State Police cars and, parked very close to a wall, a black Buick hearse.

Entering the building, one could see the outline of the State's instrument of execution - the large, crudely-made wooden gallows – standing across the damp dirt floor in the southeast corner of the building. Being in its presence, on this night, under these circumstances, chilled those present to the bone.

High atop the structure, five single light bulbs glowed dimly. Dangling from the thick heavy lumber crossbeam, there were two rough-cut ropes – both tied into a hangman's noose. Purchased earlier in the day from the Gronis Hardware store in Leavenworth, they would now serve the purpose of ending two lives.

Standing in the far corner, almost hidden in the shadows, the anonymous executioner waited. He wore a heavy, black, full-length trench coat with its collar turned up and a black, wide-brimmed hat pulled down low to hide his face.

Witnesses said that the dark figure stood silent and motionless with his hand on the handle that operated the grey metal trap door as Richard Hickock was brought into the warehouse. Several members of the execution squad said later that he stared both killers down as they climbed the thirteen steps to the top of the platform.

It had taken over five years to get them here. The multiple hearings, the appeals, and every possible legal maneuver attempted had all come down to these final few minutes inside a dirt-floored, stone-walled warehouse.

Chapter 24

Warden Sherman Crouse read Hickock the death warrant before he climbed the steps. Six prison guards stood atop the gallows. Asked if he had any last words to say, the prisoner responded, "Yeah, I guess I do." Looking toward several Kansas Bureau of Investigation agents, he said, "I don't have any hard feelings. You're sending me to a better place."

His leg shackles were then removed, and he made the climb to the top unassisted. A black hood was placed over his head, and the rope was affixed tightly around his neck, with the knot positioned behind his left ear. When he was standing at the center of the heavy steel trap door, a sudden motion by the executioner opened it and, at age 33, Richard Hickock's life came to an abrupt end.

Prison physician Dr. Robert Moore stepped forward, listened for a heartbeat and pronounced him dead at 12:44 a.m. The rope was cut and the noose was removed.

Undertaker Davis Molding transported the body to Davis Funeral Home, keeping the hood in place. Awaiting its arrival was a doctor from the Kansas University Medical Center. Both eyes were removed, according to Dr. Lawrence Hyde, Director of the Eye Bank, and taken to Kansas City, where they were transplanted to a woman and a man, both unidentified.

Perry Smith was brought into the warehouse at 12:56 a.m. and, standing below the gallows, was asked if he had any last words to say. "Yes, a word or two," he responded. "I think it is a hell of a thing that a life has to be taken in this manner. I think capital punishment is legally and morally wrong. I would like to apologize for what I have done but it would just be meaningless."

After removing Smith's leg shackles, the prison guards stepped back and watched the condemned man struggle to climb the thirteen steps to the top, where Chaplain James Post was waiting. As he finally stepped onto the platform, he could be seen nervously chewing gum. After spitting it into Chaplain Post's hand, Smith was placed over the center of the steel trap door. The black mask was pulled over his head and the noose was tightened in place.

In the final few moments of the condemned man's life, Chaplain Post said aloud, "The Lord giveth and the Lord taketh away. Blessed is the name of the Lord. May the Lord have mercy on your soul."

At 1:02 a.m., Perry Edward Smith dropped to his death. The official pronouncement came at 1:19 a.m., again made by Dr. Robert Moore. Then, after slowly descending the thirteen steps from the gallows, the executioner walked silently past those in attendance, exited through the large warehouse door, slipped into a black Cadillac and drove away into the darkness. The phone rang at the funeral home, and Davis Mulden drove back to the prison to pick up another body.

In the research and study for this book, the authors felt that the most accurate firsthand account of what transpired was recorded for history by long-time newspaper reporter William H. Brown of the Garden City Telegram. It was entitled "Cold, Crude, Casual, and Impersonal", and we quote it in its entirety here:

"As cold as the sheets of steel stacked on the warehouse floor. As casual as the prison guard leaning against a pile of lumber. As impersonal as the hangman, whose expression never changed under his broad-brimmed hat. As crude as the very gallows it is exacted upon. This is capital punishment in Kansas. I witnessed it being carried out on two men in the early hours of this morning. I know it happened but was mesmerized into a state of unreality by the total insignificance of the surroundings.

The gallows at the Kansas State Penitentiary at Lansing have long stood in the southeast corner of a general warehouse just outside the prison walls. Inside a large vehicle door stands the instrument of legal death in Kansas. I almost failed to see it as I entered the large, chilled room only minutes before Richard Hickock was brought in. The two new ropes hung from a cross beam about eight feet above the platform. There were no chairs for prison officials and others who witnessed the hangings. We stood in small groups or wandered about, trying to disguise apprehension and emotion with casual conversation or forced nonchalance.

An act of almost total formality put the one formal act that of the warden reading the warrants to the condemned men-incongruous to the proceedings. There was no last mile walk for the prisoners. Each was brought by car into the warehouse and emerged only a few steps away from the gallows' thirteen steps. The trap was sprung with an unsuspecting suddenness. The victims reached the end of their ropes with a sudden neck breaking snap in full view of any of us who wanted to look. There was no squirming or utterances from the bodies. Death was not official until several minutes later, but to the victims, life ended instantly.

The stark reality of what I had witnessed came later after I had left the improbable surroundings of the executions and had sat down to my typewriter and telephone to tell the story of two deaths to the readers and listeners of a society that has yet to grasp the complete answer to crime and punishment. Perry Edward Smith and Richard Eugene Hickock will not kill again. This is the only certainty that came out of this damp, chilly, unforgettable night."

CHAPTER 25

The sun rose at 6:07 a.m. on Thursday in Garden City. It was April 15, 1965 – the day after the executions – and the streets bustled with activity. The morning newspaper would confirm what so many had wished for over the last five long years. The two men who had confessed to and been convicted of the most brutal mass killing in Kansas history were dead. In conversations at kitchen tables, in coffee shops, at barber shops and on street corners, many voiced relief that the whole process was finally over. Many others expressed a deep satisfaction.

Meanwhile, as word spread through Holcomb, the quite little town showed little reaction. The morning regulars at the Hartman Café sipped hot coffee and listened to others read aloud from the Garden City Telegram the account of what had happened the night before. As the last of the group drifted away, a quietness fell over the little gathering spot.

It seemed that time had healed little, but life would have to move on for the townspeople. The deep scars left behind by the events of that November night in 1959 under a Kansas moon could never be understood or forgotten and would remain in their hearts and on their minds for all time.

History notes that only days after the murders (and before the killers were known), one person had written of forgiveness, saying, "There is much resentment in this community. I have even heard on more than one occasion that the man when found should be hanged from the nearest tree. Let us not feel this way. The deed is done and taking another life can not change it. Instead let us forgive as God would have us do. It is not right that we should hold a grudge in our hearts. The doer of this act is going to find it very difficult indeed to live with himself. His only peace of mind will be when he goes to God for forgiveness. Let us not stand in the way but give prayers that he might find his peace." The author was one of the brothers of Herbert Clutter.

At 10:30 a.m. on April 15th, after a brief ceremony, Hickock and Smith were buried in plain pine cloth-covered coffins side-by-side in the same grave in section 34 of row 29 of the Mount Muncie Cemetery in Lansing. No one had come forward to claim their bodies.

RICHARD EUGENE
HICKOCK
JUNE 6, 1931
APRIL 14, 1965

PERRY EDWARD
SMITH
OCT. 27, 1928
APRIL 14, 1965

EPILOGUE

Under A Kansas Moon / The Final Chapter was made possible by the use of the Kansas State Penitentiary archive files that have been preserved and stored for historical review and study by The Kansas Historical Society in Topeka, Kansas. The Richard Hickock penitentiary file consisted of 723 pages and the Perry Smith penitentiary file was 584 pages. It's from these files that the authors were able to piece together many of the details concerning Hickock and Smith's time spent in the Kansas State Penitentiary at Lansing.

In addition to the Kansas Historical Archives, the authors also used the Newspapers Publishers Extra archives. This valuable resource made it possible for the to go back in time and research and study firsthand accounts that were reported and published just as the story was unfolding in newspapers all across the state of Kansas and throughout the United States.

Over the many years since the quadruple murders occurred, there's been much debate regarding the mental states of Richard Hickock and Perry Smith. The young men were raised and brought up in vastly different types of family settings. For Richard Hickock, his childhood had been what most would have considered to be a normal upbringing, with a mother and father who cared for him and loved him. Even though the family was not financially well off, they were respected and admired by friends and neighbors and thought of as hard-working and honest, with Christian values. Many who knew Richard personally realized that he did have some issues and problems. Very early on, he had developed a reputation as a liar, petty thief and con man.

As he moved into young adulthood, he became a pedophile with an eye for young girls. When Dr. W. Mitchell Jones performed a psychiatric examination before his trial, it was determined that he showed signs of "emotional abnormality", possibly resulting from brain damage incurred in a vehicle accident as a young man. It was also believed that feelings of social and sexual inadequacy were at the root of many of his more reckless criminal actions. In short, the examination revealed that Hickock showed "fairly typical characteristics of what would psychiatrically be called a severe character disorder."

For Perry Smith, it was almost the complete opposite. Life for him had been a complete struggle from the earliest days of his youth. Years of living in desperate poverty and the dysfunctional state of his family would contribute to deep physiological problems that would follow him for the rest of his life. Dr. Jones concluded that he exhibited definite signs of severe mental illness.

Neglected as a child, he had developed a "paranoid' orientation toward the world," and "in evaluating the intentions and feelings of others, his ability to separate the real intention from his own mental projections is very poor." Perhaps the most significant item in the diagnosis is his "poorly controlled rage—easily triggered by any feeling of being tricked, slighted or labeled inferior to others." His personality traits, in other words, most closely resembled that of a paranoid schizophrenic.

While doing the research for this book, the authors found writings by another individual whose ties to both Richard Hickock and Perry Smith are well-documented and provide what is likely the best up-close description of the mindset of the two convicted murderers in the last four years of their lives.

In April of 1965, Director of Kansas State Penal Institutions Charles "Chuck" McAtee was the man who oversaw all executions in the state of Kansas. From his memories of Hickock and Smith, we're able to get a better understanding of who they were and what they were really like.

Charles McAtee

"I grew to know these two young men as human beings rather than cold-blooded murderers," McAtee recounted. "In the public's eye, the pair were demonized as psychopathic killers. I befriended them both, but I was repulsed by the shockingly violent act that they had committed." To this day, McAtee tells of the sadness that wells up when he reminisces about the goodness he found in the perpetrators of the gruesome killings.

When he took the Director position, he decided to allow inmates on death row to have the right to write him directly. And over the next four years he maintained a pen pal-type relationship with Richard Hickock and Perry Smith.

Only weeks before the two were executed, McAtee had found it in his heart to overrule the acting Kansas State Penitentiary warden Sherman Crouse and allow the men on death row to have transistor radios and headphones. "The more I thought on it, the more upsetting it was to me that these men waiting to be executed could not even hear music. I love music," McAtee says, "and I couldn't imagine living without it. These men have been on death row for years and years and have not heard one sound of music and they are going to die."

During those long years of confinement, Hickock and Smith both did a lot of soul-searching, according to McAtee. He said Perry Smith was introspective man who tried to find peace by painting, reading, and writing. Smith created biblical images on bed sheets. He memorized a book by Thoreau on "Man and Nature". Only minutes before he climbed the gallows steps, he gave McAtee a poem he had written:

"Eternal Hope"

But he who thinks that man is bare,

disrobed by pride by force,

has not the depth of soul to share emotions at its source.

Shortly before he was executed, McAtee says, his focus was upon his relationship with his family. He had written to his wife, saying that he would like any money made from the sale of his life story after he was gone to be placed in a trust fund for his children. But in angry response, she said she didn't want to be part of anything that would remind them of their father.

Having had second thoughts about her harsh reaction, she came to the prison on the day of his scheduled execution to apologize. Warden Crouse refused to allow her access to her husband, saying "The prison is locked down. You can cut the tension with a knife in there." However, McAtee overruled Crouse and the two were able to meet face-to-face. The two stood three feet apart, not allowed to touch one another. Hickock asked about the children and told his wife to give them his love.

Richard Hickock claimed until his final hours, when he and McAtee sat together in a private room, that it was Perry Smith who had killed the Clutter family.

One mental image that McAtee can't erase is that of the executioner. He recalls the man's black shirt, boots, and heavy coat and that he appeared to have about a four-day growth of beard. He moved slowly and with deliberation, and his eyes were penetrating.

He pulled the handle with great force, swinging open the gate to eternity.

The End

Resources And Discovery

Garden City Telegram 1960

January 5,6,7,11,12,14,19,23,26,27,29,

February 3,4,9,15,19,23,24

March 2,3,7,9,11,14,18,21,22,23,24,27,28,29

April 1,2,4,5,6,7,12,13,19,23

June 3,4,9,14,20,29

July 1,5,8,12

August 26

September 3,8,20

October 11,13,18,20,24,27

November 15,16,25

December 9,10,12,29

Garden City Telegram 1961

January 6,9,25

February 1,18

March 6

April 7

July 8,28

October 6

November 9

December 1,22,23,29

Garden City Telegram 1962

January 2,4,16,18,27

April 11

June 4

July 7,9

August 28,29,31

September 11,19,27

October 5,9,17,22,24

December 10

Garden City Telegram 1963

January 2,22

February 7,18

April 17

May 27

June 1,6,20,24,26

July 25

August 2,30

October 3,7 12,14,15

November 2,20

December 27

Garden City Telegram 1964

January 11

October1

December 1,9

Garden City Telegram 1965

January 19

February 13

March 12,30,31

April 1,5,6,7,8,9,10,12,13,14,15

June 8

September 17

October 6

December 3,4,6,27

Kansas Historical Society

Richard Eugene Hickock's Kansas State Penitentiary Inmate Case File

Pages 1 through 747

These pages were removed from public view in accordance with access restrictions of K.S.A. 45-221 (A) (29) of Richard Hickock's Inmate Case File. 3, 37,38,39,40,153,154,155,156,157,158,159,201,401,405,409,547,548,549,550. 551,552,553,554,555,556,557,558,559,560,561,562,563,564,565,567,568

Perry Edward Smith's Kansas State Penitentiary Inmate Case File

Pages 1 through 772

These pages were removed from public view in accordance with access restrictions of K.S.A. 45-221 (A) (29) of Perry Edward Smith's Inmate Case File.
29,30,48,49,50,51,52,53,54,55,56,57,69,109,110,111,112,113,114,115,116,117,118,119,120,121,122,123,124,125,126,127,128,129,130,131,132,133,134,135,136,137,138,139,140,141,142,143,144,219,280,390,453,454,455,456,457,458,459,460,461,462,463,464,465,466,467,468,469,470,471,472,473,474,475,476,477,478,479,480,481,482,483,484,485,486,487,488,489,490,491,492,493,494,495,496,599,600,601,611,612,613,614,615

Other Kansas Newspapers

The Emporia Gazette

April 7,1965

June 4,1962

August 30,1963

March 28,1960

July 7,1962

March 31,1965

The Parsons Sun

April 14,1965

The Manhattan Mercury

March 30,1960

June 3,1963

May 3,1960

The Ottawa Herald

January 4,1960

May 9,1961

October 11,1960

November 15,1960

The Hays Daily News

March 24,1960

August 28,1962

February 19,1961

April 7,1960

The Leavenworth Times

January 12,1960

October 9,1963

July 8,1962

March 30,1965

The Wichita Eagle

January 8,1960

April 15, 1965

The Lola Registry

March 18,1960

Articles

Rolling Stone Magazine – March 21, 2017 (In Cold Blood Killers Lost Memoirs: What we know)

The New York Post – November 17,2017 (The Real-Life Horror Behind "In Cold Blood")

CPSIA information can be obtained
at www.ICGtesting.com
Printed in the USA
BVHW081606300323
661446BV00007B/771

9 781732 739499